MAD AND DIVINE

MAD AND DIVINE

Spirit and Psyche in the Modern World

SUDHIR KAKAR

THE UNIVERSITY OF CHICAGO PRESS • CHICAGO AND LONDON

Sudhir Kakar is a psychoanalyst and the author of many books, including *The Analyst and the Mystic: Psychoanalytic Reflections on Religion and Mysticism*; *Intimate Relations: Exploring Indian Sexuality*; *Shamans, Mystics, and Doctors: A Psychological Inquiry into India and its Healing Traditions*; and *The Colors of Violence: Cultural Identities, Religion, and Conflict*, all published by the University of Chicago Press.

The University of Chicago Press, Chicago 60637
The University of Chicago Press, Ltd., London
Penguin Books India Pvt. Ltd., New Delhi India
© 2009 by Sudhir Kakar
First published in Viking by Penguin Books India 2008
All rights reserved. Published 2009
Printed in the United States of America

18 17 16 15 14 13 12 11 10 09   1 2 3 4 5

ISBN-13: 978-0-226-42287-9 (cloth)
ISBN-10: 0-226-42287-9 (cloth)

Library of Congress Cataloging-in-Publication Data

Kakar, Sudhir.
  Mad and divine : spirit and psyche in the modern world / Sudhir Kakar.
      p. cm.
  Includes bibliographical references.
  ISBN-13: 978-0-226-42287-9 (alk. paper)
  ISBN-10: 0-226-42287-9 (alk. paper)
  1. Psychoanalysis and religion. 2. Spirit. 3. Spirituality. 4. Osho, 1931–1990. 5.
'Brug-smyon Kun-dga'-legs-pa, 1455–1529. 6. Gandhi, Mahatma, 1869–1948. 7.
Freud, Sigmund, 1856–1939. Zukunft einer Illusion. I. Title.
  BF175.4.R44K36 2009
  201'.615—dc22

                                                                              2009006030

♾ The paper used in this publication meets the minimum requirements of the
American National Standard for Information Sciences—Permanence of Paper
for Printed Library Materials, ANSI Z39.48-1992.

CONTENTS

I feel myself obedient to 'spirit,' knowing that from it alone come the things that justify life—things, in Nietzsche's words, 'transfiguring, exquisite, mad, and divine.'
—Jacques Barzun in *A Stroll with William James*

INTRODUCTION

$\mathcal{F}$or a long time, any engagement with the spiritual in psychoanalysis as also in the academic study of psychology has been regarded with suspicion and dismissed as an esoteric activity that need not be taken seriously. In our scientifically shaped mentality, the spiritual was believed to exist only as the Fata Morgana of the naive eye. This was a natural consequence of the rationalist view of humans, dominant since the Enlightenment.

Our times, though, seem poised to witness the resurgence of the romantic vision.[1] In psychology, the romantic view of human life underlines the importance of the spiritual by conceiving life as a quest. There are many obstacles and difficulties on the way, but if the seeker persists then he or she will be rewarded by a union with a higher power or the Spirit.[2] In contrast, the rationalist vision is sceptical of all higher powers and exalted aims of life and likes to show that all gods have clay feet. The romantic vision is also more spiritual in emphasizing an intimate connection between humankind and universe, between self and not-self. The rationalist, on the other hand, insists on an enduring separation between the two. He looks down at the romantic view as a scientifically wrong and philosophically confused reaction to the objective rift between mind and nature. For the rationalist, the romantic is engaged in a futile and regressive revolt against the 'bad news' of Enlightenment: separateness.[3]

I must note here that, as a broader intellectual and social current, the romantic resurgence is more characteristic of Western societies than of most non-Western ones where the romantic vision never lost its ascendancy over the rational. Or, more accurately, the *Ur*-romantic vision of non-Western societies has generally remained oblivious of separateness and thus differs from the Western post-Enlightenment romantic sensibility, which has been struggling to overcome the rift even as it remains exquisitely aware of it. In fact, with the spread of modern scientific and technical education in the non-Western world, the movement is in an opposite direction as educated professionals enthusiastically embrace the rationalist vision of Enlightenment. This trend is perhaps most visible in China[4] and, to a lesser degree, also in modern India where the romantic view, including its excrescences of occultism and superstition, still holds considerable sway.

It is instructive to remember that even in the West, in spite of the attacks by the rationalists and the scientific and technological successes of the post-Enlightenment world, the romantic vision did not completely disappear but continued to persist in embattled enclaves. To give just a few examples: in philosophy one can think of Kant versus Hume, in science of Einstein versus Watson, and in my own discipline, psychoanalysis, Ferenczi and Jung, and more recently Kohut, can be said to represent the romantic position against a rationalist Freud. In anthropology, the divide cuts through each anthropologist where the participant anthropologist, identifying with and often idealizing the culture he is studying, struggles against the empiricist and detached observer within himself, seeking a balance which, depending on his life experience, is apt to be skewed in one or the other direction.[5]

I am, of course, aware of the oversimplification involved in the use of such binaries as romantic and rational. The romantic and the rational are not necessarily oppositional. A complex mind will be guided by both the visions, the romantic enlivening and lending a 'poetic' sensibility and sentiment to reason while the rational vision guards against the sentimental excesses to which the romantic is all too susceptible. And since differentiation precedes integration, it may well be that the Enlightenment's project to differentiate itself from its past by rejecting romanticism is due for a revision that will begin to integrate the two views of man and his world.

What are some of the signs of the romantic resurgence? Recent developments in social neurosciences and evolutionary psychology, for example, which, as we shall see later in Chapter V, highlight an innate altruism in human beings, or the serious questioning of the *Homo economicus* model of man acting selfishly out of self-interest in economics, can be seen as part of the romantic revival. Such findings are more supportive of Rousseau's view of man as intrinsically good, a 'noble savage', rather than Hobbes's darker vision of man as basically self-centred.

The quickening of the altruistic impulse is also evident in the wider social arena; the flourishing of NGOs, including some on a global scale, such as Medecins sans Frontier, Oxfam or Amnesty International. The unprecedented rise in charitable giving which is not limited to one's own community but embraces the whole of humanity is another signpost on this road.[6]

In Western societies, there is also a widespread and very

visible quest for 'authenticity', a notion closely associated with Rousseauan romanticism. As the anthropologist Charles Lindholm has shown, the search for personal and collective authenticity has become omnipresent in modern life. It is what we look for the most in such diverse areas as art, music, religious life, or even in travel and cuisine.[7]

What are the implications of the romantic revival and the probable integration of the romantic and rational for the pre-eminently Western discipline of psychoanalysis? Let me begin with an anecdote.

In 1994, I was honoured with an invitation from the Foundation for Universal Responsibility, the foundation set up by the Dalai Lama from his Nobel Peace Prize award, to have a dialogue with His Holiness in New Delhi. The subject of the dialogue was Buddhist and Western psychology and I, as a psychoanalyst, was asked to represent the viewpoint of Western psychology.

What I remember most vividly about the dialogue is an exchange when the topic of hatred came up. I gave the orthodox psychoanalytic view. There is something wrong with the person if he cannot hate. There is also something wrong if the person cannot stop hating. A mature person should be able to hate but also capable of transcending hatred. 'No, no!' the Dalai Lama exclaimed. 'This is not true of Buddhist psychology.' He then proceeded to tell the story about his friend, a spiritually advanced lama who was incarcerated in a prison in Tibet and tortured by the Chinese. After many years, the lama managed to escape and reach Dharamsala, the home of the Dalai Lama in India.

'How was it?' the Dalai Lama asked his old friend about his long years of imprisonment.

'Oh, twice it was very bad,' the lama replied.

'Were you in danger of losing your life?' the Dalai Lama expressed his concern.

'No. Twice I almost *hated* the Chinese!'

Of course, the psychoanalytic gloss on hatred applies to a Tibetan as much as it does to a Westerner. The aspect of Buddhist psychology which the Dalai Lama had brought into the discussion was an introduction of the spiritual into the purely psychological.

Spirituality, like culture, has many definitions and yet manages to give a sense of familiarity to most of us. For me, the spiritual occupies a continuum from moments of self-transcendence marked by a loving connection to an object—nature, art, visions of philosophy or science, the beloved in sexual embrace—to the mystical union of the saints where the sense of the self completely disappears. The spiritual, then, incorporates the transformative possibilities of the human psyche: total love without a trace of hate, selflessness carved out of the psyche's normal self-centredness, a fearlessness that is not a counter-phobic reaction to the fear that is an innate part of the human psyche. Yet spiritual transformation is not a once for ever achievement even in case of enlightened spiritual masters and saints. It remains constantly under threat from the darker forces of the psyche. One is never *not* human—'Twice I almost hated the Chinese.'

A spirituality that does not take into account and engage with the complexities and dynamic nature of the psyche, in which our bodily life plays such an important part, will fail to touch people who are not incurably romantic. It will re-main, in the psychoanalyst Heinz Kohut's felicitous phrase, experience-distant rather than experience-near. Equally, a psychology that refuses to recognize the potentialities of the psyche, of its possible extension into the realm of the spirit, a psychology which contents itself with Freud's healing offer of replacing hysterical misery with common unhappiness, does not provide enough emotional sustenance to modern man.

This book of essays, then, may be seen as a small contribution to the coming integration of the spirit and the psyche in the evolving psychology of the person. To address a human being as a whole, we need both psychoanalysis as the 'hermeneutics of suspicion' and spiritual thought as the hermeneutics of idealization. To focus only on the spirit is to hold in contempt the body that makes us human. At the same time, to treat a human being as nothing but the body is to commit the same offence of fragmentation, the denial of wholeness.

The 'spirit' in this book is not the 'luminous cloud' of the mystic that floats ethereally in mysterious regions of the human stratosphere but one that swirls among the crags of human passions—above all, desire and narcissism, which line our depths. It is a book about the interplay, at times playful, at others deadly serious, between spirit and psyche, between the spiritual and the 'flesh made subtle'. It is about moments of creativity and transformation when the spirit cools the fire of desire or thaws the ice of self-centredness. What I have tried to do in these essays is to look at this interplay and these moments in different contexts: in religious ritual, in healing traditions, both Eastern and Western, as also in the lives of some extraordinary men—Osho, Gandhi and the Buddhist saint Drukpa Kunley.

CHILDHOOD OF A SPIRITUALLY
INCORRECT GURU: OSHO

$\mathcal{I}$ first met Rajneesh, later known as Bhagwan ('Blessed One', 'Incarnation of God') and still later as Osho, in 1971 in the rapturous accounts of a visit to his Poona Ashram by a young German woman who had been in psychotherapy with me for six months. She had been 'spiritually transformed' by what she had experienced there, she declared, and was unsure whether she needed to continue therapy. I was curious and envious, not necessarily in that order. Over the next decades I followed the meteoric rise and fall of perhaps one of the best-known, and certainly the most notorious, gurus in the spiritual bazaar of the 1970s and 1980s.[1]

Rajneesh's Poona Ashram was at the centre of a spiritual movement that had successfully spread to Europe, North America, Australia and Japan. At one time, his Western disciples, primarily from a social and cultural elite—members of European aristocracy, lawyers, doctors, writers, artists, academics and other professionals—outnumbered by far the Indians who came for enlightenment to the 'sex guru' or the 'guru of the Rich' as Rajneesh had come to be known. By 1981, over 40,000 had been initiated as 'sanyasins'. These were not the traditional Indian sanyasins who renounce the world, leave their families and take vows of non-possession while they devote themselves to their spiritual search. The commitment demanded of the Rajneeshis, as his disciples were called, was limited to using the new names Rajneesh gave them at the time of the initiation, dressing in 'sunrise' colours (orange-red at first but later, pink), wearing a necklace with 108 beads and a locket containing a picture of Rajneesh, and continuing an appropriate practice of meditation.

Rajneesh loved to shock the media which, in turn, loved to be shocked by this bright-eyed, high-domed, lushly bearded imp, whose admirers considered him one of the wisest men of the age. Lurid stories circulated about his large, sprawling ashram in Koregaon Park in Poona. There were reports of a widespread use of drugs and rampant prostitution by Western female sanyasins. Orgies of group sex were said to be on the daily menu in the ashram. A deeply conservative Indian society was scandalized by the unrestrained sexual goings-on as much as by Rajneesh's mockery of the Indian establishment and his ridiculing of Indian icons. Morarji Desai, the puritan prime minister and the self-confessed daily imbiber of his own urine who came to power in 1977, was an easy target for Rajneesh's barbs. Rajneesh's followers, successful and intelligent people who, like their guru, had little interest in ideology and no respect for authority, might have enjoyed his descriptions of Gandhi as a 'masochist', a 'pervert' and a 'Hindu chauvinist', or of Mother Teresa as a 'charlatan' and 'hypocrite', a religious politician hiding behind the facade of helping the poor.[2] But many Indians and, more important, the Indian government were not amused. Hefty tax arrears were slapped on the commune and dark hints were thrown out on investigations that had been or were soon going to be launched into its financial affairs.

Rajneesh's response was to pack up and move the ashram to a small town in Oregon in the United States which he renamed Rajneeshpuram. His mission, he proclaimed, was to lead his followers to the higher states of consciousness and transform the world. Freed from the distorting conditioning of society, families and politics would become obsolete in the new world. Living in harmony and pursuing spiritual aims, the Rajneeshis would become the nucleus of a new race of human beings that would emerge after the nuclear holocaust he predicted would take place at the end of the twentieth century.

Rajneesh's Oregon stay was a disaster. The guru became more and more withdrawn, taking drugs, inhaling nitrous oxide, watching videos in his darkened room and emerging only occasionally to ride in one of the ninety-two Rolls Royces donated by his followers. His few trusted lieutenants who ran the Oregon commune became increasingly paranoid in the unsympathetic environment of the American West. Listening devices were planted in the quarters of those suspected of disloyalty, weapons were hoarded, obsessional and bizarre measures to protect against AIDS were taken and, finally, a campaign to poison suspected traitors inside the group and those outside who were thought to be hostile to the ashram was initiated. Rajneeshpuram was shut down when these illegal activities came to light. Rajneesh tried to flee the country but was arrested while boarding his flight. He was finally allowed to leave after pleading guilty to two felony charges. Some of his closest associates who had run the Oregon Ashram were sent to prison. Rajneesh finally returned to Poona after his efforts to set up the ashram at other locations failed because of the worldwide notoriety he and his movement had acquired. Suffering from various allergies and chronic asthma, Rajneesh died in Poona in 1991. He was fifty-nine.

∽

Rajneesh can be regarded as a pioneer in the globalization of spirituality and Rajneeshism as one of the first global brands in the spiritual marketplace. There have been other Indian gurus before him who took their spiritual wares to the West but their 'product' had remained recognizably Indian, comparable, say, to the export of traditional Indian handicrafts to a specialized niche market. Rajneesh's 'product', though inspired by Hindu and Buddhist Tantra which attach spiritual significance to sex, was crafted through techniques that were eclectic in nature. It owed as much to healing practices of American Indian shamans and the West Asian Sufi orders as to New Age psychotherapy techniques of transpersonal psychology which were coming into vogue in Europe and especially in the United States.

Rajneesh was not a 'sex guru' although, like Michael Foucault, he too believed that a person's sexuality revealed his or her essence, or as he put it, 'the attitude towards sex is a very symbolic attitude; it shows everything about your whole life'.[3] It would also be doing him injustice to believe that the attraction of his movement lay in the provision of orgiastic sex under the garb of spiritual striving. At the time of a flourishing 'counterculture' movement in the West, the 'Age of Aquarius', 'flower power', marijuana and LSD, one did not have to spend a fortune to travel to India, risk diarrhoea and other infections, just to get laid. By itself, sex was 'stupid', Rajneesh maintained; its spiritual significance lay in producing mindlessness or the silence of the mind that made true meditation possible. The orgasm was a door into silence, into 'the secret that there is no secret'.[4] It was the stillness and meditation after the intercourse which was the real object of the feast although Rajneesh's critics insisted on mistaking the appetizer for the main course. His other appellation, 'the guru of the rich', was more deserved. Rajneesh was definite in maintaining that only those who were comfortably off, who did not need to toil to fulfil their material needs, were receptive to their spiritual nature; or to adapt a well-known quote from the German playwright and poet Bertolt Brecht (*'Erst kommt das Fressen, dann kommt die Moral'*), 'Food first, then spirituality.'

Rajneesh's 'religionless religiousness', a spirituality without adherence to any creed, demanded a deprogramming or deconditioning of the mind. It required a transcendence of the personal past through an erasing of the markings on the blackboard which had been scribbled over again and again in the course of growing up by such cultural institutions as the family, the school and official religions. Rajneesh's philosophy of liberation emphasized a rejection of all conventional values. It highlighted direct, ecstatic experience, a knowing through intense feelings (hence the importance of sex) and acting in the world according to the dictum 'Be absolutely selfish' or, in other, somewhat more palatable words, 'The most basic and the most fundamental commitment is to love oneself.'[5] This is a far cry from most other spiritual trends. One of the most visible icons of contemporary spirituality, the Dalai Lama, states flatly, 'Paying attention to one's own needs is a producer of suffering; cherishing others a giver of happiness.'[6] The mansion of spirituality indeed has many rooms.

Rajneesh used various techniques for the deconditioning of the mind. The primary one with which he began his mission in 1971 was Dynamic Meditation. This involved letting one's body go without restrictions in a group setting in the presence of the guru. To the accompaniment of pulsating music, disciples let their bodies dance and gyrate in any manner they liked. They shouted, laughed, sobbed, rolled on the ground till a coordinated climax with strong sexual overtones was reached.[7] This was followed by communal breathing exercises and sitting quietly in meditation. Modern minds cannot be quieted by old meditative procedures requiring silence and immobility, Rajneesh asserted. The unstill mind needs to be exploded, an explosion that lets out all pent-up emotions. Only after such an active release could modern man reach a state of natural silence.

Over the years, other techniques to foster the disintegration of social constraints and personal identity were added to the repertoire offered at the ashram. Western psychotherapists of varied persuasions—practitioners of Reichian Body Work, Gestalt therapy, Primal Screaming, Past Life Regression and other 'humanistic' therapies that were being developed in the counterculture of the West of the 1970s and 1980s—joined Rajneesh and were given free rein to search for ever more effective ways to uncover the 'true, inner self'. Inevitably, 'therapy intensive' groups involving group sex became a part of the repertoire. Often, with the removal of the lid from the cauldron of instincts, overt violence and untrammelled sexuality ran riot in these quasi-therapeutic groups where physical injury and psychological trauma were not uncommon.

But more than Rajneesh's philosophy or their experiences in therapy groups, his followers held that it was Rajneesh's presence that had the power to give them the ecstasy of transcending all boundaries. His ability to induce euphoric states in his disciples carried a conviction of his divinity that was impervious to scepticism and disbelief.

There is little doubt that Rajneesh was a fascinating, charismatic figure. It was a charisma infused with great charm, an irresistible combination. For whereas charisma fascinates and awes, charm, connected (also etymologically) to magic and spells, seduces. Almost everyone, disciples and non-believers alike, who attended his discourses, testifies to his charisma that carried them—the sceptics perhaps only temporarily—to a plane of enchantment beyond the commonplace reality of ordinary lives. Warm, playful, humorous, Rajneesh's voice and especially his eyes are most often described as 'hypnotic'. In a study of Rajneesh's charisma, the sociologist Charles Lindholm has given a vivid description of the effect he had on his audience:

> His performances were expressive improvisations which moved, without pause or doubt, from highly abstract philosophical reflections to obscene jokes and racist remarks that were designed to shock his audience. They were also caught up in the exhilaration of his rapidly changing moods, his intonations and dramatic pauses, his potent rhetoric . . . As he caressed the audience with his voice, shifted emotions and rhetoric with fluidity, and used his expressive hands to counterpoint his remarks, Rajneesh gave the faithful a sense of being carried onto a higher level of existence, both immediate and transcendent.[8]

t Rajneesh self-consciously prepared for his
ces as does an actor for his role. In later life,
he would us̤ ...ake-up, wear rich robes that accentuated his
broad shoulders and jewel-studded caps that hid his baldness.
The setting for his discourse was as carefully prepared as
was the selection of music and his dramatic entry and exit at
the venue in one of his Rolls Royces.

The contradiction between authenticity and theatricality
in Rajneesh's character is not the only one in a man teeming
with contradictions. He is described by his followers as
incredibly warm but also remote, as someone capable of great
empathy but also of complete detachment and indifference.
He could be bitingly cruel, as we saw in his comments on
Gandhi and Mother Teresa, but on rare occasions he was
also capable of magnanimity and genuine admiration. The
'masochist' Gandhi, for instance, had a beautiful smile and
'an immense capacity to feel the pulse of millions of people
together'.[9] And Krishnamurti, whose hyperintellectuality
induces a migraine headache in everyone who listens to him,
is also the author of First and Last Freedom, 'one of the
greatest books ever written'.[10]

Rajneesh's own books, over 400 of them, compiled by
disciples from his talks, showcase a vast and eclectic
erudition. They are highly readable, often poetic. Studded
with some striking insights, illustrated by dramatic parables,
they also display his talent as a gifted storyteller. At the same
time, his books have many ideas borrowed from philosophers
and spiritual teachers of the world which Rajneesh blithely
appropriates without attribution. They also contain some
outlandish assertions, for instance, that Hindus had been to
North and South America long before Columbus and that

Arjuna, the famous archer of the epic Mahabharata, was married to a Mexican girl.[11]

There are many other contradictions: the guru who rejects all authority and preaches complete freedom himself exercises totalitarian control over his disciples; the messiah of sexual love who exalts intercourse between man and woman as the highest manifestation of life force was himself reported by many in position to observe him at close quarters as a voyeur who liked to watch couples, especially two women, make love and preferred to masturbate aspiring female disciples, preferably those with large breasts.[12] Rajneesh was indeed of the same stamp as the individuals William James writes about in whom there is a fusion of superior intellect and 'psychopathic temperament', creating geniuses who 'do not remain mere critics and understanders with their intellect. Their ideas possess them, they inflict them, for better or worse, upon their companions or their age.'[13]

Rajneesh was, of course, supremely aware of his contradictions and indeed revelled in them. Consistency for him was the mark of fools and Rajneesh may have been outrageous, but rarely foolish. Yet if there was one trait in his personality that seemed to be without its attendant shadow, it was a truly inordinate self-regard, an astonishing grandiosity, at least in his public pronouncements and persona. Normally, we feel repulsed by the boastfulness, self-aggrandizement and disdainful dismissal of others in which exaggerated narcissism manifests itself in a person. A braggart irritates us, because we feel his insensitivity, his lack of connection with us as he goes into raptures of self-infatuation. We feel, and rightly so, that he is using us only as a mirror to keep the image of an idealized self intact, an admired self-representation he needs for his feelings of well-being. Rajneesh, on the other hand, remained acutely aware of his audience and what they were eager or willing to believe. Many of his improbable claims and fantastic stories about his past and his 'previous lives', as we shall see below, were first narrated in the small circle of his closest devotees who believed that 'Bhagwan [Rajneesh] . . . has traveled all the paths, all the highways and byways open to any man through the aeons of time. He has played all the roles, has seen through all the games, done everything, been everywhere, and now He is a living statement of total fulfillment.'[14] The claims of such grandiosity in someone of average talent most often leads to bitterness and whining complaints of having been denied his due by 'society', 'enemies', 'fate' or whatever else. The exuberant grandiosity of someone like Rajneesh, though, who is endowed with superior gifts and what appears to be unshakeable self-belief, can be vital for his accomplishment in becoming a messianic figure.[15]

Grandiosity had been a part of Rajneesh since early childhood and remained with him, undiminished, till the end of his life. ('But I had nothing to be modest about!' I can hear Rajneesh protest with a glint of mischief in his eyes.) Let us take only one example, Rajneesh's account of his birth and his 'previous lives'.

In his last birth, 700 years ago, Rajneesh was a great spiritual master. Seekers from all over the known world flocked to him. Three days before he was to die or rather be finally liberated from the cycle of births and deaths, he was assassinated by a disciple. (The man was once again to be his sanyasin in the ashram.) Rajneesh was in deep meditation when he died the last time around.

I died consciously, hence I had the great opportunity to be born consciously. I chose my mother and father.

Thousands of fools are making love around the earth, around the clock. Millions of unborn souls are ready to enter into any womb, whatsoever. I waited seven hundred years for the right moment, and I thank existence that I found it. Seven hundred years are nothing compared to the millions and millions of years ahead . . . I chose this couple, just simple villagers. I could have chosen kings and queens. It was in my hands. All kinds of wombs were available, but I am a man of simple tastes: I am always satisfied with the best.[16]

Rajneesh's other lives, too, were no less distinguished. Another 700 years earlier, he had been great friends with Bodhidharma, the famed seventh-century Buddhist monk who brought Buddhism to China and Japan. The two travelled together for three months and, though Bodhidharma had pleaded with him to stay, Rajneesh had left him to go his own way. 'Bodhidharma could not believe it. He had never invited anyone before. This was the man who had even refused Emperor Wu—the greatest emperor of those days, with the greatest empire—as if he was a beggar.'[17] His followers are the luckiest people on earth, Rajneesh said, since:

Jesus can be found again very easily. People are becoming enlightened all the time. But to find a man like me—who has traveled thousands of ways, in thousands of lives, and has gathered the fragrance of millions of flowers like a honeybee—is difficult.[18]

If I now turn to Rajneesh's early childhood to understand the major themes in the inner world of this fascinating man who marched to his own ethical drumbeat, a *Homo spirituosi* in spite of his many contradictions, tall tales and affronts to conventional morality, it is not out of any psychoanalytic reflex. Rajneesh himself would have agreed that his particular genius cannot be understood without recapturing the quality of his earliest experiences. 'The first seven years are the most important in life, never again will you have that much opportunity,' he says. 'Those seven years decide your seventy years, all the foundation stones are laid in those seven years.'[19] Or, at another place, 'unless you understand the seed you will miss the tree and the flowering, and perhaps the moon through the branches'.[20] Yet as a psychoanalyst, the kind of biographer who is more interpretive than historical, who is concerned with the hidden meanings of childhood experiences, I must also remain true to my professional dharma of going beyond the facts of his life into the heart of the man. The search for a psychoanalytic 'truth' does not compromise my memorial admiration of Rajneesh which, though, is without the idealization and reverence of a follower. Respecting his religious genius yet aware of his human shortcomings, I am heedful of Nietzsche's warning to the scholar of religion in a secular age, namely the 'boundlessly foolish naivete' involved in the 'belief of the scholar in his superiority, in the good conscience of his tolerance, in the unsuspecting simple certainty with which his instinct treats the religious man as a lower and less valuable type, beyond, before and ABOVE which he himself has developed'.[21]

Rajneesh's reminiscences of his childhood, *Glimpses of a Golden Childhood*, are compiled from notes of his talks in 1981. These were informal, rambling talks within the small circle of four or five of his most intimate and trusted associates, whom he affectionately called his 'Noah's Ark'. Since the reminiscences are compiled from the spoken rather than written word, they are not as well-organized and edited at the source (that is, by Rajneesh) as is normally the case with written communication. Indeed, often they have the quality of free association: 'That's how I am speaking. I do not know what the next sentence is going to be or whether it is going to be at all. Suspense is beautiful.'[22] As the psychoanalyst George Moraitis observes, speech tends to be more repetitive and loosely associative than writing and has a greater chance of bringing concealed thoughts into forms.[23] We see this, for instance, in the frequent repetition of the number seven at various places even in the first fifty pages of the text, as if this number is forcing itself on Rajneesh's consciousness and into his speech. The follower who had killed Rajneesh *seven* hundred years ago in a previous incarnation confessed that he had come to kill him again in his present one, *seven* years after he had been a sanyasin (p.15). Rajneesh's father was a poor man who had only *seven* hundred rupees when he was born (p.18). The famous astrologer who came to their village refused to make his birth chart because he did not think the child would survive his *seven*th birthday (p.25). Above all, the reason, I would speculate, the number seven held a special meaning for Rajneesh, and inserted itself in *Glimpses of a Golden Childhood* in different contexts, is its association with the death of his beloved grandfather when he was *seven* and which brought an end to a golden childhood that had lasted for *seven* years.

〰

As an infant, Rajneesh was handed over by his parents to his maternal grandparents who had expressed a wish to bring up their firstborn grandson, a not uncommon occurrence in the Indian context. His nana and nani were thus the only father and mother he knew for the first years of his life; in fact, later in life, imitating his father's younger brothers, he would always address his biological mother as 'bhabhi'— sister-in-law, the place of the mother in his heart and mind occupied by his remarkable grandmother.

There is an elegiac quality to Rajneesh's memories of his years with his grandparents and of the village in which he grew up. Although many factual details are inconsistent with each other—Rajneesh was never a slave to the tyranny of facts—the narrative has a ring of emotional truth. It transcends any irritation caused by the play of his imagination which invents highly improbable incidents and encounters that could not have taken place. An autobiography is a myth we create about ourselves and would like others to believe in. Not that an autobiographer does not struggle to be truthful. It is only that his striving for truth is undermined by the unconscious power of human narcissism. The highest commandment that rules autobiographical forays into the past seems to be that the memories of our life must not do any real damage to our feelings of self-worth. Notwithstanding a few admirable exceptions, this is the unacknowledged secret of all autobiographies—and of neurosis. If Rajneesh's memories of his life diverge from those of many others in their relentless self-glorification, it is only because of the implacability of this commandment in his case which forbids him to take even the slightest risk that might be a threat to self-esteem. An inner censor keeps a strict watch that memories that may compromise a lifelong project of maintaining a magnificent self intact are turned away at the gate of consciousness.

> My childhood was golden. Again, I am not using a cliché. Everybody says his childhood was golden, but it is not so. People only think that their childhood was golden because their youth is rotten; then their old age is even more rotten . . . But my childhood was certainly golden—not a symbol, absolutely golden; not poetically, but literally, factually . . . Those years are unforgettable. Even if I reach Dante's paradise I will still remember those years.[24]

The village of Kuchwada in Madhya Pradesh where Rajneesh grew up was small and remote, without a railway station, post office, school or doctor. It had a few straw huts and its only brick house belonged to Rajneesh's grandparents. Through the golden haze of his memory, it appears as an ideal world, free of conflict and turmoil. 'The village was beautiful,' he says, 'I have traveled far and wide but I have never come across that same beauty . . . Things come and go, but it is never the same.'[25] Surrounded by small hills, the village had an ancient pond with trees that were hundreds of years old around it.

Nobody could describe that pond except Basho. Even he does not describe the pond, he simply says,

> The ancient pond
> Frog jumps in
> Plop!

. . . and certainly the frogs jumped; day in and day out you could hear 'plop', again and again. The sound of frogs jumping really helped the prevailing silence. That sound made the silence richer, more meaningful . . . But the silence of that ancient pond stays with me.[26]

Raja ('King'), as the little boy was called by his adoring grandparents, was an emperor in this small world. Rajneesh remembers that his birthdays were celebrated in the same fashion as that of a king. His grandfather would hire an elephant from a nearby town and fill two big bags, hanging on either side of the elephant, with silver coins. The small boy would then ride the elephant through the village, throwing silver rupees to an awed populace. In every possible way, Raja was given 'the idea that I belonged to some royal family'.[27]

Rajneesh does not remember little Raja ever being disciplined, irrespective of the mischief he got up to, which was considerable.

> The whole day he [grandfather] would sit on his *gaddi*— as the seat of a rich man is called in India—listening less to his customers, and more to the complainers. But he used to say to them, 'I am ready to pay for any damage he has done, but remember, I am not going to punish him . . .' Once in a while I would say, 'Nana, you can punish me. You need not be so tolerant.' And,

can you believe it, he would cry! Tears would come into his eyes, and he would say, 'Punish you? I cannot do that. I can punish myself but not you.'[28]

Raja was a lonely child. He did not play with other children of the village who were regarded by his grandparents as 'dirty' and socially inferior. 'So for seven years nobody tried to corrupt my innocence; there was nobody. Those three old people who lived in the house, the servant and my grandparents, were all protective in every possible way that nobody should disturb me.'[29] And the most fiercely protective, or rather indulgent, was his grandmother. Sensitive, beautiful and strong—some would say, headstrong—the nani insisted that Raja be left alone and be allowed to be his natural self, uninfluenced by any adult. For a short while, a private tutor was engaged, but in a pattern that continued through the years of his growing up, the child would first expose and then become teacher to the man. At the end of every such encounter, Raja's uniqueness and superiority were recognized and celebrated rather than sought to be moulded by the adult—revered Jaina monks, schoolteachers, professors, the vice chancellor of the university—who initially presumed to exercise authority over the boy. He says:

That is how, without knowing it at all, I came to have the taste of Tao. Lao Tzu says, 'Tao is the watercourse way. The water simply flows downwards wherever the earth allows it.' That is how those early years were. I was allowed. I think every child needs those years. If we could give those years to every child in the world we could create a golden world.[30]

If Rajneesh remembers his grandfather as a paragon of unconditional though passive love, the love of his nani was active and energetic:

> [M]y grandmother helped me immensely. My grandfather loved me, but could not help me much. He was so loving, but to be of help more is needed—a certain kind of strength. He was always afraid of my grandmother. He was, in a sense, a henpecked husband.[31]

His nani was the reigning monarch of his soul, an extremely beautiful, 'strong woman, very strong'. The grandfather, affable and totally indulgent, was the queen's consort in the background who nonetheless represented an enclave of calmness, the quiet pole in the psyche of the little boy, a needed refuge from the fierce power of the beautiful nani: 'Beauty is always so, courageous and dangerous.'[32]

Simple, uneducated, yet independent, his grandmother had married at the age of twenty-four and from love, both unheard of in India at the beginning of the twentieth century when girls got married at nine or ten to husbands selected by their family. Rajneesh relates many incidents where she encouraged him to be rebellious, to dare all, for instance, to show a venerable Jaina monk the door if the child so wanted. She told the boy that when he was older he must visit Khajuraho, her birthplace and the site of temples with erotic carvings that still have the power to shock a sexually conservative society. When Rajneesh was in his teens, she provided him money to smoke, drink and visit prostitutes if he wanted to. Experience every experience without fear, seemed to be her message to the child, exhorting him to seek, in the poet Ernest Dowson's words, 'madder music and stronger wine'. She held before the child the vistas of his future greatness: 'Perhaps she could see something in me of which I was not aware in those days. Perhaps that's the reason she loved me so much . . . I can't say.'[33] In turn:

> I never saw a more beautiful woman than my Nani. I myself was in love with her, and loved her throughout her whole life. When she died at the age of eighty, I rushed home and found her lying there, dead . . . To put the fire to her body was the most difficult task I have ever done in my life. It was as if I was putting fire to one of the most beautiful paintings of Leonardo or Vincent van Gogh. Of course to me she was more valuable than the Mona Lisa, more beautiful to me than Cleopatra. It is not an exaggeration. All that is beautiful in my vision somehow comes through her. She helped me in every way to be the way I am. Without her I may have been a shopkeeper or perhaps a doctor or engineer . . .[34]

The striking nani, then, gifted her adored Raja, 'the king of my heart', with (in Nabokov's phrase) 'unreal estate' where nothing would ever go wrong and where, in an artistic elaboration of the child's mental state:

> You were carried and you were enveloped in the amplitude of sure protection, like a king on his throne, with his faithful bodyguards many ranks deep about him; and the landscape beyond, with its motley episodes, became the most entertaining of spectacles,

where everything was unexpected and exciting, yet where nothing could go wrong; as if your mother herself had been telling you a story, and these pictures were only the illustrations to it which painted themselves on your listening mind.[35]

Nothing could go wrong, except that everything did. Rajneesh's grandfather died when he was seven and the golden childhood came to an abrupt and traumatic end. The child returned to live with his parents in their small town and in a large, extended family with its inevitable conflicts and clamour, not to speak of the demands made on the child by school and other institutions of society to conform to their norms. For instance:

I was forced almost violently to go to school. And it was not a one-day affair, it was an everyday routine. One of my uncles, or whosoever, would take me there, would wait outside until the master had taken possession of me—as if I was a piece of property to be passed from one hand to another, or a prisoner passed from one hand to another.[36]

At school:

It was a daily routine, almost the usual practice, that I was sent to the headmaster to be punished. The captain of the class would take me to the headmaster, who used to then ask me what I had done that day. But by and by the headmaster stopped asking. I would go there and he would punish me, slap me on the face, and that was all. He did not even ask what wrong I had done.[37]

What helped the child save his battered soul from irreversible damage was the refuge he could find with his nani. After the grandfather's death, nani left Kuchwada and moved into a small house in the town so that she could be close to her Raja. Rajneesh would spend the nights with her so that she was 'not alone and by herself' and, perhaps more important though unacknowledged, that neither was he. She soothed the hurts of his day, mirrored the grandiose self now under violent attack from reality, helping him salvage the early psychological buoyancy and creativity of the child and carry them into adulthood.

I will not belabour the obvious psychoanalytic inference that Rajneesh's childhood experience led to the formation of a highly narcissistic personality, hyperempathic to his own needs and with an inordinate need to maintain the conscious experience of a grandiose self. All small children go through a phase of heightened narcissism but, if they are lucky, also move away from it in a gradual, non-traumatic manner, carrying away with them some of the uplifting triumphs of this stage: humour, creativity, aesthetic pleasure, optimism. It is only when the parental indulgence and mirroring have been intense, and the exile from the symbiotic nest sudden and traumatic, as in Rajneesh's case, that there is a strong probability of developmental arrest at this early stage of life. The longing for the lost paradise of childhood where a great self existed in a symbiosis with ideal parents becomes the central motif in the psyche, the theme song of the person's unconscious life ever after. Rajneesh's more or less conscious stance, 'I am great. I walk alone. I need no one. Others need me,' which provided a template for his later relationships with others, not only desperately needed disciples and followers to reassure him that its fictions were true but also became vulnerable to bouts of regressive longing. At the time when he was sharing memories of his childhood with his close disciples, he constantly played one old song by Noorjahan, a famous Urdu singer of the 1930s and early 1940s. He would listen to this particular song again and again, morning and night. The song (in Rajneesh's translation):

> Whether you remember or not,
> Once there was passionate love between us.
> You used to tell me,
> 'You are the most beautiful woman in the world,'
> Now I don't know if you will recognize me or not,
> Perhaps you do not remember, but I still remember.
> I cannot forget the passionate love, and the words you
>   said to me,
> You used to say your love was impeccable,
> Do you still remember?
> Perhaps not—but I remember,
> Not in its totality, of course,
> Time has done much harm.
> I am a dilapidated palace,
> But if you look minutely,
> I am still the same.
> I still remember the passionate love[38] and your words,
> That passionate love that once existed between us,
> Is it still in your memory or not,
> I don't know about you,
> But I still remember.

There is heartbreak, longing and hints of betrayal of old promises in the song that Rajneesh sings silently, again and again, through the haunting voice of Noorjahan. Is this a song to his nani? To his lost childhood? To the transience of love? Or perhaps to all of them? Here, we can sense the presence of a deeply sad and deprived core in his psyche that is split off from consciousness. Strong defences guard against the emergence of this depressed core which, however, sometimes breaks through the fortifications. On occasion, it even takes over the personality, as it did during periods of psychic breakdown in youth, especially the long stretch of psychic disintegration that preceded his spiritual enlightenment at the age of twenty-one.

In contrast to the endearing narcissism of the child and its demands to be at the centre of attention, the grandiose self of the adult arrested at the stage of infantile narcissism is infused with heightened aggression. In Rajneesh's case, this was expressed in his disdain, arrogance and frequent devaluation of others, especially of other religious teachers and spiritual preceptors. To Rajneesh, they were all worthless, 'bullshitters', not holy men but 'holy dung'. Swami Muktananda, a contemporary Indian guru with a large following, was an 'Idiotananda'.

Identifying with a grandiose self and its sense of manifest destiny, growing up without playmates or peers and hence never learning to compromise with the needs of others, bathed in parental overindulgence which rendered the internalization of 'no' impossible, was bound to lead to a lack of any self-discipline. Rajneesh was thus relatively free of restraints that would check his psyche's expansiveness and sometimes manic exuberance. Feelings of guilt and pangs of conscience that serve to regulate the behaviour of normal mortals were conspicuously absent. It is essentially the recapture of a 'remembered' total state of freedom which he elaborated in his spiritual message and philosophy with erudition, rhetoric giftedness and, above all, conviction, for Rajneesh had himself been *there*.

> So don't be worried about what you are doing; remember only one thing: what you are being. This is a great question, about doing and being. If your being is right, and by right I mean blissful, silent, peaceful, loving, then whatever you do is right. Then there are no other commandments for you, only one: just be. Be so totally that in the very totality no shadow is possible. Then you cannot do anything wrong. The whole world may say it is wrong, that does not matter; what matters is your own being.[39]

The death of his grandfather at the age of seven that marked the end of a golden childhood was not only decisive for the course of Rajneesh's psychic life. Its trauma that provided the glue that cemented the grandiose self firmly in his psyche was also vital in awakening and giving form to his spiritual strivings. Rajneesh returns to the deeply traumatic experience again and again.

> I was so attached to him that his death appeared to be my own death . . . In the very first attack of death upon my grandfather, he lost his speech. For twenty-four hours we waited in the village for something to happen. However, there was no improvement. I remember a struggle on his part in an attempt to speak something but he could not

speak. He wanted to tell something but could not tell it. Therefore, we had to take him toward the town in a bullock cart. Slowly, one after another, his senses were giving way. He did not die all at once, but slowly and painfully. First his speech stopped, then his hearing. Then he closed his eyes as well. In the bullock cart I was watching everything closely and there was a long distance of thirty-two miles of travel.

Whatsoever was happening seemed beyond my understanding then. This was the first death witnessed by me and I did not even understand that he was dying. But slowly all his senses were giving way and he became unconscious. While we were nearby the town he was already half dead. His breathing still continued, but everything else was lost. After that he did not resume consciousness but, for three days, he continued breathing. He died unconsciously.

The slow losing of his senses and his final dying became very deeply engraved in my memory.[40]

How traumatic the grandfather's demise must have been for the child and how his psyche struggled to master its attendant anxiety and the radical restructuring the death required are evident from Rajneesh's extraordinary reactions to the event. Now there is a consensus among psychoanalysts that children do not pass through the same mourning process as adults in whom a gradual and painful emotional detachment from the inner images of the person who has passed away takes place. In children the reaction to parental death in childhood is not mourning but rather a complex series of defensive phenomena aimed at denying the reality of the event. An unconscious denial, a screening out of feelings of sadness and loss ('It can't be bad if I don't feel bad!') and other responses, such as glorification and idealization of the dead parent and unconscious fantasies of a reunion, are some of the more common.[41] Rajneesh's reactions, however, went much beyond these normal responses. As an older child and youth, it was his practice to follow dead bodies that were being carried to the cremation ground. Watching people die became a hobby: 'The moment I would hear that somebody was on his deathbed, I would be there . . . and I would sit and watch.'[42] He would imitate the state of death, go to cremation grounds at night and lie there as motionless as a corpse for hours at a stretch, trying to achieve, the analyst would say, a reunion with the grandfather.

Seven years later, at the age of fourteen, convinced he himself was about to die, he took *seven* days' leave from school. He went to an old, isolated temple at the outskirts of the town and lay there 'being dead'. Spiritually, his reactions to his grandfather's death may be seen as so many efforts at detachment and indeed this is how Rajneesh interprets them: 'His death freed me forever from all relationships . . . whenever my relationship with anyone began to become intimate, that death stared at me.'[43] Indeed, St John of the Cross holds such radical detachment to be essential for travel on the spiritual path: 'The soul cannot be possessed of the divine union, until it has divested itself of the love of created beings.'[44] In line with a more modern, sceptical sensibility, the poet T.S. Eliot avers that detachment is not a choice but the only option available when human relationships have failed: 'A man does not join himself with the Universe so long as he has anything else to join himself with.'[45]

Spiritually, the most important episode of Rajneesh's life took place another *seven* years later when he was twenty-one and went through a prolonged period of psychological breakdown, his 'dark night of the soul'. It was a time of what he calls 'nervous breakdown and breakthrough' that was to be the midwife for his emergence as a spiritual Master.

> For one year it was impossible to know what was happening . . . just to keep myself alive was a very difficult thing, because all appetite had disappeared. Days would pass and I would not feel any hunger, days would pass and I would not feel any thirst. I had to force myself to eat, force myself to drink. The body was so non-existential that I had to hurt myself to feel that I was still in the body. I had to knock my head against the wall to feel whether my head was still there or not. Only when it hurt would I be a little in the body . . . For one year it persisted. I would simply lie on the floor and look at the ceiling and count from one to a hundred then back from a hundred to one. Just to remain capable of counting was at least something.[46]

The dreams of flying through which the grandiose self often exhibits its perfection[47] gave way to those of falling that reflected the disintegration of this self as Icarus hurtled down from the heights, its wings burnt to cinder:

> My condition was one of utter darkness. It was as if I had fallen into a deep dark well. In those days I had many times dreamt that I was falling and falling and going deeper into a bottomless well. And many times I

> . . . awakened from a dream full of perspiration, sweating profusely, because the falling was endless without any ground or place anywhere to rest my feet . . . My condition was full of tension, insecurity and danger.[48]

And then, as in accounts of so many mystics all over the world, at the worst point of the breakdown, after 'seven days [that] I lived in a very hopeless and helpless state', the spiritual dawn breaks through. There is 'the presence of a totally new energy, a new light and new delight, became so intense that it was almost unbearable, as if I was exploding, as if I was going mad with blissfulness'.[49]

Spiritual transformation thoroughly shakes up the body–mind entity yet does not completely rearrange the psychic furniture. Our psyche that has been developing since birth and is physiologically embedded deep in the neuronal networks of the brain cannot be wiped out by even the most powerful mystical experience. The latter may create new neuronal pathways without, however, erasing the old ones. In myriad anxious, stressful moments of daily life, and especially during long periods of psychological stress, there is an automatic regression to earlier ways. Rajneesh's 'anniversary reactions' to his grandfather's death, for instance, did not disappear with his enlightenment. The psychological effect of this death accompanied him throughout his life, demonstrating the force of its impact. There were other 'anniversary reactions' at the end of seven-year cycles, of which perhaps the best documented is the one in 1981—the year he reminisces about his childhood in such detail. This was the year when, at the age of forty-nine, he moved the ashram from Poona to the United States. Before the move, he had become more and more withdrawn, rarely showed himself in public, while his physical condition—diabetes, asthma and various allergies—worsened.

I am aware that given his reputation as a highly gifted fabulist, there will be many who will doubt Rajneesh's account of his spiritual journey. Instead, they would prefer to believe that large swathes of it are probably fabricated out of a voracious reading in mystical literature harnessed in service of a lively imagination and using the many devices of fiction, such as suspense and coincidence. Personally, I have little difficulty in holding incompatible convictions about Rajneesh's spiritual enlightenment. In other words, as a novelist fascinated with the spiritual destiny of his fictional characters, I believe what I have difficulty believing as a psychoanalyst, namely that Rajneesh *did* pass through his valley of the shadow of death before emerging into spiritual light, while at the same time the sceptical psychoanalyst in me wonders whether it was not merely a period of extended clinical depression that ended with a hypomanic episode.

Today, as we gain a more intimate knowledge of lives of saints and spiritual masters than was provided by hagiographies, we can say that the spirit when it soars often pulls up the psyche in its wake. But we also know that the spirit never completely escapes the gravitational pull exerted by the forces of narcissism, aggression and desire in the psyche. What may be essential for our gaze, however, is to attend to the vision of the spirit's soaring, not the oft-repeated tragedy of its fall.

SEDUCTION AND THE SAINT:
THE LEGEND OF DRUKPA KUNLEY

The saint is an archetypal figure of faith in world religions. In contrast to the priest, who is thought to incorporate the narrowness of religion, with its rigidities and clinging to dogma, the saint is believed to exemplify the possibilities of human freedom. Whether the saint be Francis of Assisi or Teresa of Avila in the Christian tradition, Milarepa in the Tibetan-Buddhist or Mira Bai in the Hindu tradition, the saint reveals the other face of belief—belief as a source of joy, wonder and awe. In spite of his human shortcomings and idiosyncratic behaviour that sometimes borders on the bizarre, the saint appears committed to the extension of human potentials and thus deserves the special interest and even admiration of the psychoanalyst. Given the analyst's professional orientation, however, it is natural that he finds the saint's conflict with desire, a conflict that is common to all of us, of absorbing interest. Desire, for the analyst, is more than concupiscent lust. It subsumes elements of yearning, wishing, as also of pleasure and instinctual excitement.

For many a saint, the conflict with desire takes on a singular intensity and resonance which is later revealed as essential for his or her spiritual progress. The encounter with desire is upfront in Tantra, both Hindu and Buddhist, although the erotic language used to describe similar episodes in other religious traditions hints at their universal occurrence in the story of becoming a saint. This is one such story.

∽

In 1480 CE, according to the legend, a young Tibetan man, Kunga Legpa'i Zangpos by name, now famed all over the Himalaya as Drukpa Kunley, returned home after many years of arduous monastic training. He was twenty-five years old.[1]

During his years of learning and apprenticeship, an always precocious Kunley had mastered the complete doctrine of his Kagyu lineage and diligently followed its demanding regimen. After becoming enlightened, he cast off his monk's habit, abandoned systematic yoga and meditation, and decided to lead the wandering life of an itinerant mendicant. It is this life, full of ribaldry and magic, crammed with sexual adventure and the awakening of people he meets on his travels to the truth of the Buddha, that has made Kunley the most popular saint of Tibet and a culture hero of Bhutan. He is someone who is not only revered but regarded with great affection by the peoples of the Himalaya.

Before he could begin his travels, the legend reports the following singular encounter with his mother. And since Kunley's 'biography' does not narrate any other incidents during his short sojourn at home before he leaves it to begin his wanderings, this encounter with his mother seems to be an 'unfinished' business he must complete before he can enter his destiny as the Divine Madman, a true original even among the many other bizarre holy men, the 'God's fools', who people the 'crazy wisdom' tradition of the world's religions. He is one of those saints of whom C.G. Jung remarks, 'The foolish contradiction, between an enraptured existence in a cosmic self and the loveable weakness . . . I feel drawn to this contradiction, for how can one otherwise reach wisdom without the foolishness?'[2]

When Kunley returned home, his mother, unaware of his Buddhahood, his secret identity, gave him some unsolicited but sensible maternal advice. If you want to lead a religious life, she said, you must lead a pure spiritual life, constantly devoting yourself to the service of others. If, on the other hand, you decide you prefer being a lay householder, you should take a wife who will help out your old mother in the house. As the biography further describes the encounter:

> 'If you want a daughter-in-law, I will go and find one,' Kunley answered.
>
> Matching words to the deed, Kunley went straight to the marketplace where he saw a decrepit and toothless old hag, her eyes clouded blue with cataracts.
>
> 'Old lady,' Kunley said. 'I have chosen you as my bride. You must come with me.'
>
> Since the woman, bent double with aching bones, was barely able to move, Kunley carried her home on his back. Playing the dutiful son, he then announced to his mother that he had carried out her wishes and brought back a wife. Appalled, the mother ordered him to take the old woman back.
>
> 'I could do her work better,' she said.
>
> 'Well, if you can do her work better, I will take her back to the marketplace,' Kunley good-naturedly agreed.

That night, the legend goes, Kunley went to his mother's bed carrying his blanket.

'What do you want?' asked his mother.

'This morning you said you'd perform a wife's duties, didn't you?' he replied.

'You shameless creature!' responded his mother. 'I said I'd do her housework. Now don't be so stupid. Go back to your own bed.'

'You should have said what you meant this morning,' the lama told her, lying down. 'It's too late now. We are going to sleep together.'

'Shut up and go away, you miserable man!' she swore at him.

'My knee has gone bad and I can't get up. You'd better resign yourself to it,' he persisted.

'Even if you've no shame,' she said, 'what will other people think? Just imagine the gossip!'

'If you're afraid of the gossip, we can keep it a secret,' he promised.

Finally, unable to find words to rebuff him, she said, 'You don't have to listen to me, just don't tell anyone else. Anyhow, there's a proverb that goes, "To sell your body, you don't need a pimp; to hang a painted scroll you don't need a nail; and to wither your virtue, you don't need a mat in the sun." So do it if you're going to!'[3]

Her words fell into his ears like water into boiling ghee, and he sprang up and left her alone.

Early next morning he went down to the marketplace and shouted aloud, 'Hey listen, you people! If you persist, you can seduce even your own mother!' When the whole crowd was aghast, he left. But by exposing the hidden foibles of his mother, her faults were eradicated, her sins expiated, and her troubles and afflictions removed. She went on to live to the ripe old age of 130 years.

Soon after this incident, he told his mother that he was going to Lhasa, and that in the future he would live the life of a Naljorpa.[4]

The prologue to the compilation of stories about Kunley's life, collected from oral and literary sources by a renowned Bhutanese scholar, Geshey Chaphu, is aware of the various possible attitudes with which this encounter between mother and son can be regarded: 'If you read it with shame you will perspire, if you read it with deep faith you will weep; if you read it with languor you will drool at the mouth; if a woman reads it with lust her lotus flower will moisten; and if anyone reads it and distorts it with an opinionated mind, his soul will leak into the lower realms.'[5] And since I am as wary as the next person about the danger of my soul leaking into the lower realms, let me first take the opinion of the saint's own tradition on the proper way of approaching this story.

A Tibetan-Buddhist reading would probably emphasize the following three points to help readers outside the tradition appreciate the deeper import of the story and the role life stories of saints play in the culture.

First, Kunley is not an ascetic monk but a Secret Mantra adept. In other words, he is a Tantrik. Tantra is not only infamous for the uses of sexuality in the spiritual endeavour but is also characterized by a profoundly subversive intent. Gaining currency in Indian Buddhism after the seventh century, Tantric practices aimed at overturning the caste restrictions of the Brahminical order, flouting food taboos and breaking sexual prohibitions. The almost mother–son incest in the Kunley story is not only yet another taboo to be broken but a vigorous push against the boundary of all that is tabooed, a straining against the mother of all taboos, so to speak.

Second, Kunley is a divine madman in the tradition of the eighty-four mahasiddhas ('Great Perfected Ones') who lived in North India between the eighth and twelfth centuries (in fact, he is an incarnation of one of the best known, Saraha) and of the lineage of the Tibetan saint Milarepa and his wild guru, Marpa. Like these other teachers of 'crazy wisdom', Kunley instructs through parables, songs and actions that are overtly scandalous. Kunley's actions, though, are actually meant to shock the mind of the listener or the viewer out of its conventional conditioning, rearrange its furniture so that it becomes receptive and welcoming to unfamiliar spiritual guests. The lama's incestuous offer to his mother is then only one of his many outrageous shockers that seek to open the path to Buddhahood for others. It is of one cloth with his pissing on a sacred thangka mandala (the urine is later revealed to have turned into a gold finish on the painting) or his mockery of religious pompousness and clerical self-satisfaction through unbridled ribaldry. Remember what he did at the temple of Ramoche where he found the monks engaged in a scholarly, metaphysical discussion? 'I know a little of metaphysics myself,' Kunley said, and grabbing a fistful of his own fart he opened the fist under the monks' noses and innocently asked, 'Which came first, the air or the smell?'[6]

Third, the affair with his mother is not a part of the spiritual biography of Kunley's inner life, of his 'full liberation story' that describes his meditation experiences, stages of realization and visions of past lives. Nor is it an episode in an external biography that details facts about his life and times. The stories about the Divine Madman are written in the third genre of Tibetan life-story writing, in the style of 'secret biography'. In a secret biography, Choegyal Gyamtso Tulku tells us in his foreword to the book, the saint's life is 'fully revealed in terms of his perfect activity, and there is no distinction made between external events and the inner life. The path of development has ended, and with complete abandon, the Master is seen fulfilling the highest goal . . . to give meaning to other people's lives.'[7]

I fully agree with the Tulku that this story, in conformity to the Mahayana Buddhist altruistic norms which govern the telling of life stories in Tibet, seeks to impart 'meaning to other people's lives'. I would, however, like to offer another meaning of this 'meaning'. Listened to with the analyst's third ear and interpreted by using a psychoanalytic imagination, it produces another kind of secret biography that is more indebted to Freud and the post-Freudians than to the Buddha and the Tantric masters. The psychoanalytic secret biography, too, seeks to instruct (and, one hopes, also entertain) the reader in ways which, as we shall see below, though different from the Buddhist intention, can certainly be regarded as a complementary enterprise in that it too addresses certain basic and universal human desires and dilemmas.

For my proposed reading, the Kunley stories cannot be viewed as a biography in the conventional Western sense, which demands an exclusive focus on the subject's individuality and on the intimate details of his personal life. Although the saint's originality and the vivid colours of his personality are clearly discernible, his life story also repeats some of the idealized patterns of Buddhist hagiography: an exalted spiritual lineage, precocity, early renunciation of worldly life because of disillusionment (in Kunley's case as a consequence of his father's murder in a family feud), long period of learning and meditative praxis in a monastic retreat.[8] Even some of Kunley's reported conversations are found in the biographies of other Tibetan-Buddhist masters. Thus, for example, Kunley, in answer to five girls he meets on the way to Kongpo and who ask him where he comes from and where he is going, replies, 'I come from behind and I'm going ahead.' The same conversation, in exactly the same words, is also to be found in a biographical account of another holy man, Patrul Rinpoche, with the variation that the interlocutor here is a hermit.[9] Thus although some of the incidents narrated in Kunley's 'biography' may have a basis in history, for a psychoanalytic reading it is best to view these stories as folklore rather than as part of a life history. The focus in such a reading then shifts from the hero to the audience. As stories that are shared, repeated and widely circulated, they offer us a view from inside the Tibetan-influenced cultures of the Himalayan peoples on the fantasized dilemmas in the making of a saint. Moreover, the reflecting mirror of Kunley affords them an opportunity to recognize their own hidden desires and conflicts—as also their spiritual truths and possible destinies.

In order to embark on such a reading, the analyst's attitude towards the hero and his exploits need not diverge from that of the traditional Himalayan reader who is advised to approach the reading while not sitting lackadaisically in attitudes of disrespect, keeping his mind awake and listening in relaxation with a clear mind.

To me, Kunley's encounter with his mother is an imaginative staging of a scene in the drama of sexual desire. In more psychoanalytic words, it is an unconscious fantasy that draws on the hallucinatory resources of desire itself. Fantasy, of course, is desire's chosen vehicle of self-representation, one that continues to exert a tenacious fascination over it throughout the course of human life. As the psychoanalyst Torres puts it, in creating images, spinning fantasies and raising mirages of 'what almost looks like what never existed', symbolically repeating satisfactions that can never be completed, desire seeks not only to obtain pleasure and defend against anxiety but also to open the unconscious to meanings vital for the formation, strengthening and integration of the self.[10]

In this particular fantasy, Kunley is the hero of the early childhood, phallic (as opposed to, say, the infant's 'oral') phase of desire, a proxy for the phallic magnificence longed for by the little boy—and that not only in Tibet and Bhutan. Children who see him pissing against a wall shout in astonishment, 'What an enormous cock and balls he has got!'[11] (In reply to which the lama sings them a short ditty on the difference in cock shape and size in summer and winter.)

Drukpa Kunley's exuberant phallicism has made him a fertility saint whose blessings are sought by many childless women, not only from Bhutan but also from the USA and Japan who visit the Chime Lhakong monastery he founded in the early sixteenth century. If there is any doubt about

Kunley's possession of a magical and majestic organ, his Thunderbolt of Flaming Wisdom as the text calls it, this doubt will be quickly dispelled by what Kunley's vajra[12] does to various demons, not to speak of maidens, Tibetan and Bhutanese, he meets on his travels. More than once it is wielded as a hammer to smash the teeth of male demons, thus depriving them (as we know from the language of dreams) of their potency; it makes a female demon helpless by wrapping her in its foreskin. When he enters the Demon of Wong Gomsarkha's territory where the demon had carried off all the inhabitants except an old woman, he lies down naked on the ground after giving himself an erection.[13] The demon became apprehensive at this unnerving sight, decided to leave him alone and eat the old lady instead. The lama precedes the demon to the old woman's house and assures her of his protection. When the demon came with his slaves, the lama hit him in the mouth with his phallus, knocking out his teeth. The demon surrendered and promised to henceforth follow the way of the Buddha.[14]

Kunley's phallus not only violently unmans the monsters of the child's imagination that would threaten his desire, but as the saint's vajra of illumination it also transforms evil-doers into protectors of Buddha's truth. These twin associations, the double face of the phallus, are clearly seen in another story where Kunley meets a band of merchants carrying a load of spears. The lama demands one for himself from the leader of the group. The merchant is incensed and presses the spear against Kunley's chest.

'Let's see if your spear of ignorance is as powerful as my spear of Empty and Pure Awareness,' said the lama. And he grabbed the head of the spear that was thrust at him, pulling it like elastic and tying a knot in it.[15]

Kunley's accomplishments in prescience, magical powers and ability to change shapes is the stuff of every little boy's imaginings which will allow him to assert himself, seize initiative (Erik Erikson called this the stage of 'initiative vs. guilt'[16]) and prevail in a world where the adults seem so unfairly endowed with a disproportionate amount of power. The possession of a secret identity—the Buddhahood—which would astonish people, make them grovel at his feet in awe and reverence if they were but aware of it, is a further attempt to resolve the discrepancy between the child's inner and outer worlds. It is an effort to bridge the chasm between how he often imagines himself to be and the way he is regarded by the adults, an issue that looms large as a subject of desire's imaginative works at this stage of the child's life.

Kunley's encounter with his mother is a navigation through a climactic scene in desire's fundamental plot that begins at the beginning of life, in the inaugural moments of the mother–child relationship where the child, so to speak, becomes implanted with the 'desiring substance'. It is here that the most stubborn of illusions take birth, fantasies that must be dispelled by the mystic who would travel beyond the borders of desire into the adjoining territory of the spirit. In the phallic phase in which Kunley finds himself, desire's stratagems circle around the universal taboo of mother–son incest, struggling against the boy's recognition of his sexual inadequacy in relation to his mother's adult genitals, even as he desperately seeks to undo the chagrin of his Oedipal defeat.

In Kunley's replay of the early scene, the helplessness is not that of the boy but of the woman; the sexual aggressor is the son, not the mother. Here we see desire's attempt at the mastery of a trauma by turning what was passively endured into an active enterprise, the son taking the initiative in seducing the mother to escape her overwhelming, traumatic, yet profoundly seductive presence. The unsettling part of the scene, where a carefully concealed reality of desire in the mother–son relationship breaks through the cracks of a scrupulously constructed illusory structure, is the revelation of the *mother's* own desire. The mother's acquiescence to Kunley's sexual demands is troubled more by the possibility of other people finding out about the incest than by her own horror at the breaking of a fateful taboo or the stabbing of an unbearable guilt.

The story, then, is a forgotten yet unforgettable scene of sexual desire in the mother–son relationship. It is a scene which, to adapt one of Adam Phillips's memorable formulations on the psychoanalytic process, the lama must 'remember in a way that frees him to forget',[17] where he recreates the original dilemma of desire in order to relinquish it and move on in his spiritual journey. The most unacceptable part of this dramatic enactment, the answer to a question that the lama had not even thought of asking, has to do with the nature of the mother's sexual wishes in relation to the son. Wanting to shock her out of her ignorance— psychological and spiritual—Kunley is shocked by the indication of her sexual interest in him; 'her words falling like water into boiling ghee', spattering the psyche with drops of burning oil, shattering the self-possession of even an enlightened saint. In spite of the intrusion of the unexpected in this carefully staged revival of incestuous desire, the therapy ends well, for both mother and son. Her hidden secret exposed, the mother's 'faults were eradicated, her sins expiated, and her troubles and afflictions removed'.[18] The son, on the other hand, unshackled from his Oedipal desires and conflicts, freed of what I have elsewhere called 'maternal enthrallment', [19] can now embark on his mature travels—sexual and spiritual.

The spiritual autobiography of Swami Muktananda, a Hindu god-man who became a celebrity on the Western guru circuit during the 1970s, provides another example of a saint's attempt at a *mindful* resolution of the revived conflict around incestuous desire.[20] Although he was careful not to behave publicly in a way that would shock the moral sensibilities of his largely middle-class Indian following or antagonize his Western followers whose images of saintly conduct was inevitably influenced by their Christian and Jewish backgrounds, Muktananda is not unrelated to the crazy wisdom of Drukpa Kunley. As an adept of Siddha Yoga, whose Tantric core he shared with the spiritual practice of his Tibetan-Buddhist predecessor, Muktananda was also a distant heir to the legendary eighty-four great siddhas. His own guru Nityananda (d. 1961), who had lived a life free of all conventional constraints on dress and deportment, was as well known for his irascible unpredictability as for his mystical perfection.

The second part of Muktananda's account of his spiritual progress is a remarkable document that describes his meditation experiences over many months in meticulous detail. As he traverses through different stages of consciousness, Muktananda gives us fascinating descriptions of his many visions, both beatific and horrifying. He tells us of bodily changes and emotional roller-coaster rides, of ecstatic heights and mental collapses that accompanied his meditations. And then, during the course of this spiritual journey, there is an utterly baffling occurrence which threatens to end the journey before its goal has been reached.

In the preceding days, Muktananda's Siddha Yoga meditative praxis, with its focus on a total absorption in identification with the guru, had been proceeding smoothly. A 'divine red light', accompanied by intense feelings of joy or the quieter ones of bliss, had become an enduring presence.

> Then a ruinous kind of meditation came to me—a sensual meditation, a meditation of desire. How disgusting it was! I saw the red light but its color had changed. It was my size and was shining like the soft rays of the morning light in the east. All the love and intoxication I had felt in meditation left me. My identification with Nityananda went away. My Guru worship and the mantra *Guru Om, Guru Om* disappeared. Instead, in their place came a powerful sexual desire. Who knows where it had been hidden all this time? It completely possessed me. I was amazed at the uncontrollable strength in my sex organ, which was, after all, only a lump of flesh. It became intensely agitated . . . Now everything was directed outward, toward sex, sex, sex. I could think of nothing but sex! My whole body boiled with lust, and I cannot describe the agony of my sexual organ.[21]

Muktananda goes on to describe the visual accomplice of desire's sensual assault.

> When I shut my eyes, I saw, right in front of me, a beautiful naked girl inside the red light. Even though I

didn't want to see her, she appeared . . . If I shut my eyes, she was there, and if I opened them, she was there. What could I do? Whom could I tell about my embarrassing situation? It was all being forced on me against my will. How powerful was the craving of my sexual organ! I was overcome with remorse and could not meditate anymore, because I would remember this sexual desire. I felt frightened, ashamed, and discontented . . .

Afternoon came, and I meditated a little, but the same naked woman appeared. At times she laughed, at times she smiled, at times she stood, at times she sat. I could not bear to see her anymore. The earlier visions, which had calmed and purified my senses, which had brought a rush of love to my heart so that I drank supreme ecstasy, had all disappeared, leaving their very opposite. My sex organ would become stimulated, excited, powerful. Other shameful things would happen, which would make me get up quickly from meditation.[22]

Muktananda is now quite distraught. Again and again, he tries to meditate, absorbing himself in his guru and, for a while, is even successful in his effort.

I began the worship of Gurudev and became immersed in identification with him . . . I felt very happy. Then, at this moment of happiness, the goddess appeared, naked except for jewels that adorned her . . . My mind became very restless. My sexual organ became agitated with great force. I opened my eyes. I still saw her outside. Tearing my loincloth, my generative organ dug forcibly

into my navel, where it remained for some time. Who
was raping me like this?[23]

The answer comes from a voice from within when he begins
meditating in a different hut after he had been wandering
around the countryside for a few days, restless and in despair.
The voice tells him to open an old cupboard that is in the
hut and read the book lying on a shelf.

It opened at a page describing the very *kriya*s that had
been happening to me. When I read it, I was supremely
happy; in a moment, all my anguish, confusion and
worry disappeared. I now understood that everything
that had been happening to me was the result of the
full blessing of my Gurudev, Bhagwan Shri Nityananda.
It was all a part of the process of *siddha mahayoga*; it
was the way to spiritual realization.[24]

Another great siddha whom Muktananda approaches for
further explanation tells him that the woman he saw in his
meditation was Mother Kundalini. She had appeared to expel
his sexual appetites so that henceforth he could remain free
of lust. It was his false understanding of the nature of woman
that had confused him, Muktananda realizes. The mother
goddess takes all forms, naked or clothed, and he should
have remembered the goddess, the mother of Yoga, when he
saw the naked woman.[25] After this crisis, Muktananda's
spiritual practice progresses quickly.

Reading this account of perhaps the most formidable part
of Muktananda's spiritual progress, I cannot help but
remember one of the momentous passages in Freud's writings.
In 'A Difficulty in the Path of Psycho-analysis', he writes:

Man feels himself . . . to be supreme within his own mind. In certain diseases . . . thoughts emerge suddenly without one's knowing where they came from . . . these alien guests seem to be even more powerful than those which are at the ego's command . . . or else impulses appear which seem like those of a stranger, so that the ego disowns them . . . The ego says to itself: 'This is an illness, a foreign invasion.' . . . Psycho-analysis sets out to explain these uncanny disorders . . . and is right to say to the ego, in the end: 'Nothing has entered into you from without; a part of the activity of your mind has been withdrawn from your knowledge.[26]

Muktananda's meditative stage of consciousness is not a disease, nor is his vision an illness or 'uncanny disorder'. Yet subscribing to the essential truth of Freud's observation, a psychoanalyst, even one such as myself who is respectful and sympathetic to a person's spiritual life and strivings, is compelled to ask, perhaps rhetorically, whether Muktananda's vision of the mother goddess is not *also* a resurrection of another, more psychological than spiritual encounter—that of the child with his earthly mother? In other words, the saint's vision is spiritual *and* psychological at the same time since it also incorporates a surprise meeting with the mother of childhood, a mother who is now blurred, retouched and reproduced in the son's work of imagination. The next question is: 'Which mother?' For although initially the naked goddess poses a riddle to the meditating saint, she is obviously not a female demon of infantile fantasy, a projection of the infant's own devouring hunger and destruction fantasies. Neither is she the monstrous Sphinx—

Sophocles called her 'the bitch with hooked claws'—who would throttle and devour those who cannot read her riddle. Nor is the divine female Jung's 'terrible mother', nor the Medusa who petrifies anyone who meets her eyes.

The clue to the identity of the goddess—an identity buried in the early years of the saint's life history—lies in her bewitching beauty . . . and the effect it has on our hero's penis. She is the mother of his early childhood—the Oedipal phase in psychoanalytic language, a period associated with the dawn of consciousness and identity—when the little boy's discovery of his penis, and the exquisitely unsettling sensations it produces, coincides with a fascination with the mother's luminous beauty. Hers is a beauty that enlivens the boy's senses but also sets them afire, threatening to immolate self-possession. The vision of the goddess, then, is a 'screen memory', hiding behind it a slew of memories from a period when little Muktananda's love affair with his mother—the undisputed deity of his inner world—was at its peak, where, in the full flowering of desire, the mother promises the son portents of a great future. Yet, at the same time, her promise of phallic magnificence to the child is subject to the undertow of a specific fear, the small boy's dread of losing his budding masculine identity, his little penis disappearing in the dark and deep cave of his mother's femininity.

The assertion that the vision of Mother Kundalini has its origins in Muktananda's psychic substratum and is given form by the incestuously charged representation of his real mother is not a reductionist reading of a spiritual drama. I have no intention of reducing the visions of the naked goddess to hallucinations or hypnagogic mirages. As the psychoanalyst and scholar of religion Antoine Vergote has observed, the power of a religious-spiritual signifier (the goddess Kundalini in this case) is needed to lend an imaginary form the density of flesh.[27] It is Muktananda's ardent belief in the reality of Kundalini which adds a 'coefficient of visible reality' to the representation. And although neurotic hallucination and mystical vision follow the same process of transforming thought into imaginary form, there remains a radical difference between the two. In the mystic—and this, as we saw, is true of Muktananda's visions of the red goddess—a stream of conscious thought keeps a check on the fascination aroused by the imaginary image, preventing it from completely taking over the subject's consciousness.[28]

How does Muktananda deal with the bewitching mother who, like the witches in *Malleus Maleficarum*, 'can do marvelous things with regards to the male organ',[29] even making it lead a separate existence from its putative owner? Unlike Kunley's strategy of reversing the roles of mother and son in the mise en scène of the seduction fantasy, Muktananda chooses an altogether different route. At first, he struggles against being sucked into the vortex of sexual desire by calling on Nityananda, attempting to recreate and preserve the identification with his guru. In the apt though inelegant language of psychoanalysis, Muktananda tries to recover the omnipotent paternal phallus of childhood as a protection against the overpowering maternal imago and the dangerous desire to merge with her. Here, the Indian mystic is not unlike a hero of Greek mythology, Ulysses, who defends himself against the siren song, resisting its fatal temptation by asking to be tied to the mast of a ship, the paternal phallic emblem which would protect him.[30]

With the support of the guru phallus, Muktananda then takes the next step of modifying the object of desire through a process of its idealization. The deeply shocking and unsettling sexuality of the mother is transformed into the lyricism of a transfigured maternal goddess promising nurturance, protection and spiritual greatness.

We find this idealization, of mothers in general and his own mother, Kusumeshwari, in particular, elaborated in the dedication to his spiritual autobiography. After expressing remorse that he left home at the age of fifteen to embark on his quest, thus causing his mother much grief and pain, Muktananda writes:

> Children owe a great debt to their mothers. Mothers feed their children with their own vital juices; they give up their own happiness and find it in their children's happiness. What must my mother have done for her dear son! What ideas and plans she must have had for me! How many gods and goddesses she must have propitiated for the sake of my happiness.[31]

He then goes on to talk of other women who took over his mother's caretaking role during his adult years.

> During the period of my sadhana ['spiritual discipline'], my temperament was extremely peculiar and arrogant. Yet how much love these mothers gave me! They really are my revered mothers, who did so much for me. With hearts full of pure and selfless devotion, they fed me and put up with my disposition . . . As I remember them, I beg them to forgive me generously. I bow to

you, mothers, with all my heart, seeing you each as my own mother, the one who gave birth to me.[32]

Does the erasure of desire's lineaments from the visages of mother and son, staged so dramatically during the practice of a spiritual discipline, mean that the mystic has been successful in ridding himself permanently of all sexual desire? Or is Muktananda's idealization of the mother merely an unconscious stratagem, serving the purposes of repression (with its implication that, some time or the other, the repressed always returns) rather than a genuine sublimation? Muktananda would perhaps claim the latter, asserting that after such a radical incision of desire, any seemingly sexual behaviour on the part of the saint is no longer sexual in intent but has quite different aims than how they appear to the unenlightened bystander. My concern here, though, is not to examine this claim in the light of Muktananda's later life, especially in the reported sexual experiments of his old age[33] (when conceivably a certain decompensation took place and some of his early defences no longer worked), but the elucidation of the part played by seduction in the making of a saint.

Seduction, we saw above, in the cases of both Kunley and Muktananda, is a major roadblock set up by desire in the way of spiritual progress. Seduction is one of the 'primal fantasies', an *Ur-phantasie* which Freud believed constituted the foundations of psychic life irrespective of the unique, personal experience of different individuals.[34] As such, these 'essentials' must be somehow negotiated by an aspiring mystic who seeks a radical restructuring of his or her psychic organization. This seems especially true of seduction which may have a privileged position among the primal fantasies, at least in some forms of yogic practice such as that of Siddha Yoga. Building on Freud's assertion that the mother not only carries out her nutritional function in caring for the child but also passes on the basic models of erogeneity, Jean Laplanche emphasizes that the psychic reality of seduction is a joint creation of parent and child.[35] In other words, the mother's seductiveness in the mother–son relationship, which can disturb the equanimity and composure of even the highly evolved saint, is neither a consequence of a real, concrete seduction nor a pleasurable, wish-fulfilling yet terrifying fantasy of the son alone. The ubiquity of seduction lies in the vital presence of a sexual unconscious in the adult, the mother in this case, and its communication to the child through many of her physical ministrations. For instance, Laplanche observes that Freud's notion of the child's experience of satisfaction at the mother's breast or the Kleinian construction of the breast as a 'good' or 'bad' object, a representation for the child, overlooks the fact that the breast is primarily sexual for the mother, a part of her sexual life as an erogenous zone.[36] As such, the breast transmits a message to the child and this message is primarily sexual. Such messages are frequently unclear or opaque to its recipient and transmitter alike. Laplanche likens their reality to a parapraxis, a slip of the tongue.[37] Put simply, there is much more seduction going on in the mother–child interaction than is consciously realized by the mother . . . or son. We must remember, though, that seduction in such a relation is asymmetrical. The sexual message originates from the adult, although as a slip of the tongue, and we would err if we looked at it only as the son's dream—or as actual abuse by the mother.

I should emphasize here that the replay of maternal seduction in the spiritual quest of a saint is just that, a play, a dramatic enactment of a compelling fact-fiction ('faction') which might have been but was never real. In cases of actual seduction of the son, episodes of a hypnoid state are not uncommon during psychoanalytic treatment. This altered state of consciousness, though, has the character of a hysterical symptom, a reminiscing without remembering, to which the patient clings with great tenacity, clearly loath to give up his symbiotic tie with the seducing mother. Thus in a case reported by Austin Silber, the patient recalled taking a daily afternoon nap from the ages of three to five lying next to his mother. In the fateful sexual play that followed, he would become sexually excited, the pulsations of his body akin to the pulsing of his penis during ejaculation as an adult. The mother would take the child's hand and move it over her vulva. After a while she would either grasp his leg and rub it across her genitals or lift his whole body on top of her. Holding him firmly by the hips she would then move his body over her moistened sex, at first gently and then more forcefully, making soft crooning sounds or, occasionally, singing a nursery rhyme. The little boy remembered struggling as his discomfort mounted. His squirming would have the effect of further exciting the mother, increasing the vigour with which she manipulated his body against her vulva. He would flail out with his arms and eventually his body would go limp while his mother's efforts at erecting the son became even more frantic. The boy would then become deeply hypnotic.

In the analytic sessions, this patient often moved from tenseness and extreme restlessness to a somnolence lasting for several seconds in which he would have an indistinct 'dream', accompanied by an erection, and then awaken feeling alert and completely refreshed.[38]

The altered state of consciousness experienced by a victim of real seduction is related to Muktananda's vision of Mother Kundalini like the foggy, black-and-white photograph of a painting bursting with brilliant colours is related to the original. It is as a weak dribble to a massive waterfall . . . but related nevertheless.

In conclusion, we saw in the accounts of spiritual development of a medieval Buddhist lama and a modern Hindu guru that a resolution of the crisis brought about by the resurgence of the seduction of the early mother–son relationship was vital for their spiritual progress and that some spiritual disciplines recreate this seduction with a hallucinatory intensity. At least some saints must pass through the valley of desire, where the largest shadow is cast by the entrancing mother of memory.[39] The symbols that help the saint emerge from darkness—the vajra of Kunley, the goddess Kundalini of Muktananda—are simultaneously sexual and spiritual, in contrast to our normal human lot where they remain trapped in the field of desire alone.

DESIRE AND THE SPIRITUAL QUEST:
THE LEGEND OF DRUKPA KUNLEY
(CONTD)

*A*fter the encounter with the mother, Kunley's quest, which like all quests is a self-chosen exile from home, begins with his asking passers-by in the market square about the place where he can find the best *chung* (Tibetan beer) and the most beautiful women. Asked where he is going, he answers, 'I am looking for a fifteen year old girl. She has fair complexion and soft, silky, warm flesh, a tight, foxy and comfortable pussy, and a round smiling face; she is beautiful to behold, sweet to smell, and she has sharp intuition. In fact, she has all the signs of Dakini.'[1]

His audience, expecting the lama to ask about the best-known monastery or the most pious monk, is scandalized. What kind of saint is this who is only interested in women and alcohol! Kunley's brazen talk of chung and tight pussy perhaps makes them miss the full import of our hero's last sentence.

In Tantric Buddhism, a dakini is a representation of uncommon psychic experience. She is also a female embodiment of power and knowledge. As the former she is the inspirational force of the awakened mind, the bodhicitta, who reveals herself at an appropriate moment in the seeker's spiritual progress. In her latter aspect, a dakini represents the knowledge, the Buddha-wisdom, that helps the seeker overcome his ignorance. The exalted status of the dakini in Tantric Buddhism is a far cry from the way she is viewed in the more orthodox schools of Buddhism where she embodies the defilements or undesirable passions, the *klesha*s, that afflict a seeker. Her exalted status in Tantric Buddhism parallels the process in which the buddha–dharma–sangha trilogy as a beacon to the faithful was expanded in Tibet by the new trilogy of lama–yidam–dakini: spiritual teacher–tutelary deity–mystical female partner. Sexual intercourse with a dakini, then, is also a course in spiritual perfection. Aptly, the Mahasiddha Saraha, now reincarnated in Kunley, was also enlightened by a dakini who revealed to him the ultimate nature of his own mind.

Sunchok, the fifteen-year-old girl with all the signs of a dakini, is the first of eventually 5000 women Kunley will awaken to Buddhahood through and with the help of sexual passion. The stories of the lama's sexual peregrinations through the length and breadth of the Himalaya follow a single pattern. When the lama first appears in a girl's life, he usually sings her a *gur*, a poetic song expressing personal religious insight (in Kunley's case, also awash with sexual double entendre). The girl's heart fills with devotion once she recognizes his spiritual perfection and she willingly submits to his advances in which she receives 'more pleasure and satisfaction than she had ever experienced'. Once the sex is over and the lama is preparing to leave, the girl discovers within herself the valued Buddhist sentiment of 'disgust with the world' and insists on following him as a way of initiating her own spiritual life. Kunley initially demurs but finally gives in. Soon, though, after the girl has become established in her own meditation in a lonely spot he selects for her, the lama leaves her to continue on his travels. His lesson to the women seems to be that no person can ever be the ultimate source of happiness or quench the thirst of love of another human being—only the realization of Buddhahood can.

For an enlightened master like Kunley who must have compassion for all sentient beings, who would husband the world rather than any single woman, all women are potential sexual and spiritual partners. For him, there can be no romantic exclusivity, sexual or spiritual. The very brevity of his sexual affairs as well as their incandescent intensity are an illustration of the importance Tantric Buddhism places on sex as an aid to enlightenment while simultaneously making it transparent that, like all authentic experiences, sexual passion too is fleeting and impermanent. Before we continue with the story of Kunley's sexual spirituality, we need to digress briefly on the role sex plays in Buddhist spiritual practice.[2]

In the Theravada school, prominent in Sri Lanka, Thailand, Laos, Cambodia and Myanmar, sexual passion, like the other kleshas (aggression, ignorance, envy and pride), is a producer of suffering and an obstacle to spiritual growth. But unlike the ascetic regimens of many other religious traditions—one need only remember the prodigious feats of self-discipline of some Hindu yogis and the Christian desert fathers—Buddhist practice does not seek to overcome the obstacle of sexuality by force, root it out by the hair, so to speak, but to work on its gentle transformation. In the *shamatha* practice of sitting meditation without objective or goal (identical with the Zazen of Zen Buddhism), sexual lust and longing are experienced fully under the aegis of a watchful yet benign awareness so that these powerful emotions can be transformed into a kind of raw sensitivity and vulnerability and, ultimately, into the tenderness and empathy of the 'awakened mind', the bodhicitta.

The Mahayana ('great vehicle') school, prevalent in China, Japan and some other countries, transforms sexuality into a bridge to other beings through the practice of the virtues (*paramita*s) of patience, discipline, generosity, effort and meditation. And indeed given the dangers sex poses to our self-possession, sexuality becomes a perfect place for the exercise of the paramitas. The psychic dangers of sex are many. Its insatiability, with its waves of violent, consuming hunger, threatens the loss of those we hold dear. Naked in our desire, we are vulnerable to disapprobation, mortification, rejection. Challenging the keepers of the social order and guardians of its taboos, we tremble at the punishment fitting the crime, emasculation, or more generally an unsexing. Worse still for many is the spectre of relentless self-punishment—searing, burdensome guilt.[3] The practice of paramitas should help neutralize the dangers, help sexual passion evolve from unheeding lust into the fundamental Mahayana Buddhist virtues of loving friendliness (*maitri*) and warm compassion (*karuna*). The goal is a refinement in the alchemical transformation of sexual passion, now leading from the generalized goodwill of maitri and karuna to sensible and effective action that helps others. Mahayana altruism, then, evolves from passion; its agape is not separate from but grows out of eros.

In Vajrayana, the school of Tibetan Buddhism, sexuality

is a universal, creative energy. Here the Theravada and Mahayana practices are not denied but incorporated and sought to be further transcended. The Tantric practices of Vajrayana are said to purify the klesha of passion (as they do the other kleshas) so that it reveals itself as a form of enlightened wisdom, a Buddha-mind. In its enlightened form, sexual passion is *padma*, the lotus, a beautiful flower that grows in muck. As long as sexuality does not contradict the altruistic commitment of Mahayana or the Theravada precepts against its ignorant and harmful expression, it is a welcome and powerful aid on the way to spiritual perfection in Vajrayana.

Saints do not have to be Tibetan Buddhist or representatives of other 'crazy wisdom' traditions of the world to be passionate. The equation of a saint with placidity bordering on bloodlessness, of someone who is unmoving and unmoved by human passion, is highly misleading. The Christian saint Teresa of Avila, although she was silent on the source of a saint's passionate nature (and would probably have rejected the notion of a sublimated sexuality as its root), holds passion to be integral to saintliness. Persons who are immersed in God, she tells us, will not be cold and sterile in their relationships with others. 'No,' she proclaims, 'they will love others much more than they did, with a more genuine love, with a greater passion and with a love which brings more profit; that, in a word, is what love really is.'[4] The Tantric master, too, is nothing if not passionate but, unlike the Christian saint, acknowledges and welcomes the creative fire of sex as the source of all passion. But to continue with our story:

The brief account of Kunley's encounter with what the tradition describes as his favourite woman (although an enlightened master should have no favourites) is a good illustration of the pattern of Kunley's spiritual-sexual 'philandering', interweaving frank, even bawdy, sexual elements with elevated philosophical ideas.

'At Pachang, Drukpa Kunley rested outside the house of the girl called Namkha Dronma and waited for her to appear. The girl saw him from a window, and although she had never set eyes on him before, the very sight of him awoke her spiritual potential . . .' The girl then sings him a song where she beseeches him to stay for a while and give her perfect understanding. The lama is impressed and, knowing that she is a suitable candidate for initiation, he too replies in a song, saying that he can give self-realization to only those who have devotion:

'So if you wish to gain Buddhahood now
    'First show your faith and devotion.'
    Namkha Dronma served him tea, chung and food.
'You are very beautiful, Namkha Dronma,' he told her.
'Aren't you married yet?'
    'I am still a virgin,' she replied.
    'Yah! Yah!' he said assuringly. 'We will do it slowly!'
    Still drinking chung he took her inside. Before sitting down on the carpet he said, 'First the carpet must be consecrated. Lie down here!'
    She shut the door. 'Will it be painful?' she asked.
    'No, but if you have any butter, bring me a little.' He smeared a little butter on his Thunderbolt and then made love to her. 'Did it hurt?' he asked her when they had finished.

'I can't say whether it was pleasure or pain,' she replied, 'but I know I feel better now than ever before.'

'What were you thinking?' he asked.

'I wasn't thinking anything,' she told him. 'I was just feeling.'

'That is how it should be,' he assured her. Then he gave her instruction on the Great Bliss of the Lower Door. He stayed with her several days, revealing the essence of the Perspective of the Most Profound Reality and then sent her to meditate in the mountains . . .[5]

Using the frame of sexual seduction, this brief narrative conveys two basic Tantric Buddhist notions on spiritual enlightenment. The first is the importance of complete faith and unquestioning devotion to the master, including the welcoming of his sexual advances—if that be the master's wish. This utter trust in the master's intentions, the suppression of any doubt concerning the propriety of his actions, and the weakening of the woman's own judgement on how she feels about and reacts to the master's sexual proclivities—since such a judgement, she is told, is but a remnant of the 'ego' that needs to be surrendered for progress on the spiritual path—is now increasingly questioned. In the contemporary world, sensitized by feminist movements to the potential and actuality of sexual abuse in power relations, the issue of spiritual teachers having sex with their disciples is no longer a private affair and continues to bedevil the reputation of some Hindu gurus and Tibetan masters, especially those who have journeyed westwards since the 1970s.

One of the most highly respected spiritual authorities, the Dalai Lama, condemns the instances of a spiritual teacher having sex with his disciples and observes that the fundamental guide to ethical action is the presence of compassion for all beings.[6] Since the disciple is emotionally vulnerable, the consequences of sexual seduction of the disciple by the teacher can have unforeseeable consequences and thus goes against the fundamental Buddhist precept of loving consideration. How would he then react to the accounts of Drukpa Kunley's sexual adventures and seductions? Kunley, the Dalai Lama says, was a saint who could foresee the consequences of his actions through his psychic powers. He was cognizant of the long-term benefits of his seductions. He had attained the non-dual state of 'one taste'. In this state all the experiences were the same to him; he could enjoy excrement and urine just like the finest food and wine. Traditionally, the practice of Tantric sex is permitted only to practitioners who can match Kunley's spiritual state. 'As for the teachers nowadays who sleep with many students,' His Holiness laughed and said, 'if you put into their mouth some urine, they will not enjoy.'[7]

The second idea is encapsulated in Namkha's answer to Kunley's question as to how she experienced sexual intercourse—'I can't say whether it was pleasure or pain' and 'I was not thinking anything. I was just feeling.' This is 'one taste', a spiritually valuable attainment of non-discrimination, a neither-this-nor-that, a mental state that is an intense feeling devoid of all conceptualization. As Stephen Butterfield describes it in his personal account of Buddhist Tantra, 'One taste means saying neither yes nor no to any experience, but living thoroughly whatever happens, with full awareness of its texture, qualities, trajectories, echoes and aftereffects.'[8] Of course, even an enlightened saint occasionally stumbles, deviates from this ideal of 'one taste'. Kunley, his biography affectionately allows, is no exception. Although the enlightened master would like to awaken the spiritual potential of all women by making passionate (but detached) love to each of them, his body famously rebels in the case of an eighty-year-old woman who had been invoking him in her prayers for protection from affliction and pain. When Kunley reveals to her that he is the object of her prayer, the woman challenges him, 'If you are the real Drukpa Kunley, let's have sexual intercourse!'

But the woman is too old and Kunley cannot get an erection.

'Perhaps it is better if we have spiritual intercourse through a few well chosen words,' the woman says finally, crestfallen.

A much relieved lama hastens to oblige her.[9]

Moving from the realm of spiritual to that of sexual, with one neither standing for nor reducible to the other, both proceeding along parallel lines but with strong 'elective affinities', we see that the lama is very much a 'phallic' saint— lively and active, adventurous, curious, full of mischief and swaggering with initiative.[10] The story of his journey through the Himalaya is then naturally pervaded by phallic imagery, in contrast, say to the Odyssey where the yearnings and longings of a man returning home lead to a predominance of 'oral' imagery incorporating the wishes to rest, to sleep, to be soothed, to be fed, to be reunited.[11]

One of Kunley's principal phallic qualities, accounting for much of his popularity among the Himalayan people, is his use of wit and guile to puncture the pretensions of the pompous, take down a peg or two the influential and the powerful. In the case of Tibet, these were overwhelmingly a part of the religious aristocracy, chiefly the venerable abbots of famous monasteries. His outrageous statements and actions are greeted with hearty laughter by laymen but earn him black looks from the monks. One day, while in Lhasa, Kunley decided to go and see Tsongkhapa at the temple of Ramoche outside the city. The great man was renowned for his towering intelligence and regarded as a veritable Manjushri, the Buddha of intelligence. The monks, however, refused Kunley admission to Tsongkhapa's august presence since he had not brought a formal offering with him. The lama protested that he was unaware of this rule and would gladly come with an offering the next time. The monks, however, were adamant.

'If it is absolutely necessary,' offered the lama finally, 'I have this fine pair of testicles given to me by my parents, will they do?'

Incensed by his impertinence, the monks chased him away.

After receiving a good deal of gold as a token of gratitude from a couple he had helped to have a son, Kunley again made his way to the Ramoche temple.

'Do you still have your balls as offerings?' asked the monks.

'No. This time I have gold to offer him,' responded the lama.

'Then you can gain audience immediately.'

'Yah! Yah!' laughed the lama. 'If one has gold to offer, the way is immediately opened.' And he thought to himself that he should open these monks' eyes for them.

Ushered to the Presence, he proceeded to prostrate to the box of gold intoning the words:

'I bow to the Illuminator of our Darkness,
The Crown of Tibetan Sages, Tsongkhapa!
· · · · · · · · ·
I bow to the lover of wealth and comfort—
May this offering of gold bring joy to his heart!
I bow to him whose eyes turned from a poor and
    lowly votary
When I visited you last year with no offering!'

'O Lord of Beings, Kunga Legpa, you speak truthfully
and it is good to hear you,' Tsongkhapa said in reply.
He knotted a protective thread and gave it to the lama,
asking him to accept it as a blessing. 'You need nothing
more than this,' he said. 'Wear it!'

The lama accepted the token and withdrew. 'What
shall I do with this thread?' he thought to himself. 'It is
not comfortable to wear around my neck. I have no
pocket to put it into, and I don't want to carry it in my
hand. Better I tie it around my penis which is quite
clean and has nothing to carry.' So he wrapped it around
his penis and went to the market.

'Look! Look!' he shouted. 'If you have fifty pieces of
gold you can gain audience with the Buddha
Tsongkhapa himself. He may even give you one of
these!' and he waved his member with the thread around
it in the air.[12]

There are many such Rabelaisian subversions of authority.
Instead of bowing to a stupa in the middle of a monastery
Kunley kneels between the thighs of a woman, the place from
which 'all good and evil enter the world'.[13] In another
monastery he breaks wind 'like a dragon' in the middle of

DESIRE AND THE SPIRITUAL QUEST 71

the assembly hall, much to the disgust of the monks who cover their noses, though to the delighted giggles of the novices, with the result that even today the back rows where the novices sit have a smell of incense while the front rows of the elders are never reached by the holy scent.[14]

Kunley's view of official religion and the ecclesial establishment is well captured in one of his songs:

> Happily I am no common ritualist Lama
> Gathering followers, power and wealth,
> Without time to experience the fullness of life.
> Happily I am no scholarly monk
> Lusting for novice lovers,
> Without time to study the Sutras and Tantras.
> Happily I do not stay in a Mountain Hermitage
> Entranced by the smiles of nuns,
> Without time to ponder the Three Vows.[15]

His own religious vision is deeply humanist, valuing not the ritual and esoteric elements of Buddhist faith but its central message of compassion. Do not strive to breathe the thin air of spiritual heights, the lama seems to say. That is a difficult enterprise often marked by self-deception. Instead, concentrate on the easier task of working to eliminate the negative parts of your own nature. It is easier to abjure what you have than attain what you do not.

Kunley's message is unequivocal: what is important in religion is not its outer trappings but the substance—an innocent heart full of devotion. To an uneducated old man, who longs to learn a refuge prayer that will prepare him for death, Kunley teaches the following lines, to be recited whenever the old man thinks of the lama.

I take refuge in an old man's chastened penis, withered
   at the root, fallen like a dead tree;
I take refuge in an old woman's flaccid vagina, collapsed,
   impenetrable, and sponge-like;
I take refuge in the virile young tiger's Thunderbolt,
   Rising proudly, indifferent to death;
I take refuge in the maiden's Lotus, filling her with rolling
   Bliss waves, releasing her from shame and inhibition.[16]

Whenever the old man thinks of the lama, and this is often,
whether in the company of visitors or dining with the family,
he starts to recite the prayer. The family is shocked. It declares
him mad and banishes him to live out the rest of his days in
the hayloft in the roof. When he dies, people find a sphere of
rainbow light on the bed where the corpse should have been
lying. The monastery, known as Khyimed temple, stands at
the place where the old man, reciting Kunley's prayer of
refuge, found enlightenment.

The second half of Kunley's journey, leaving the highlands
of Tibet for the valleys of Bhutan, shows a marked change,
even a reversal, in the flow of unconscious fantasy structuring
the narrative. The fantasy now becomes more archaic. If a
journey symbolizes the interpretation of a life, then Kunley's
psychic life seems to proceed in a reverse direction, from
maturity to infancy, from phallic sexuality to pre-Oedipal
imaginings. The female figures he now encounters are often
witches, female demons or serpent ogresses—all of them
infantile images of the powerful and sexually devouring
mother. These maternal images and the castration fears of
the little boy, his dread of losing his penis (and budding
identity), are frank and unadorned. When a female demon

appears in the form of a fish-ogress, Kunley bravely states that he is ready to face even its most frightening form as the 'giant yoni [vagina]-ogre'.[17] Here, as in the images of Medusa's head or Gorgon, there is no disguising the dread of the mother's genitalia.

The sexually passionate engagements of his younger days with demure young women with tight pussies are now more and more memories of the past. The struggles with the maternal monsters are violent and harsh. Kunley's success with women no longer lies in awakening potential dakinis to their Buddha nature through sexual intercourse but in binding the malevolent power of frightening females and thus relieving the inhabitants of the valleys from the terror they inspire. The lama's encounter with Long Rong Demoness is illustrative of the new trend in his psychic life.

This particular demoness had been subdued by Kunley during his earlier travels. She now reigns over a valley through which the lama is riding his horse on his way to his favourite Namkha. The gigantic female is 'straddling the valley, her breasts flying in the wind, her hair trailing on the ground, and her organ gaping between her thighs'.[18] She refuses to let Kunley pass. Kunley takes his erect penis in his right hand and holding it aloft he grasps one of her drooping breasts with his left hand. He then sings a song to her which extols his own courage; he is even 'fearless in your vast vagina, Devil Woman'.[19] The demoness retreats and hides in a big boulder but our hero thrusts his penis into the rock and pulverizes it into smithereens. Here we have a symbolic renewal of Kunley's power through sexual intercourse with the mother who, rather than the father of later childhood, is fantasized as the source of all power. That the demoness Long Rong stands for the mother of fearful fantasy becomes apparent when she gives up the struggle, bowing to the fantasized power of the little boy's phallus. The child's fantasy succeeds in carrying out a transformation wherein she once again becomes the protective and nurturant 'good' mother, who explains her recent angry and fearful visage:

> Drukpa Kunley, conqueror of your own mind!
> I am the elemental consort you left behind.
> When you opened yourself to human girls
> I confess I was vengeful and jealous.
> I beg you to be patient with me.

Then she appeared in the centre of the river looking sad and repentant. She took a yak horn full of rice and chung and offered it to the lama gracefully, repeating her vow never to harm living beings.[20]

If, psychologically, the Odyssey is a portrayal of a man's journey from his infantile relations with female figures to his adult, 'genital' relationship, Kunley's travels took him in an opposite direction. His phallic insouciance at the beginning of his quest, with its overvaluation of the penis, an attempt to achieve power through identification with the paternal phallus, seems to be in retreat in the latter part of his life. What we see in Kunley's old age is a revival of unconscious fantasies at the dawn of consciousness wherein the mother, both terrifying and nurturant, threatening and protecting, was perceived as the source of all power. Such regressions, we saw earlier, are not uncommon in lives of saints and gurus who, as they age, often act out the resurgence of these pre-Oedipal imaginings, to the consternation, if not horror, of their followers, and the ill-concealed glee of their detractors.

ࡡ

Drukpa Kunley is perhaps the only saint in the religions of the world who is almost exclusively identified with the phallus and its creative power. The undisguised representation of his erect organ is painted on the walls of many Bhutanese houses and he is traditionally represented in thangka paintings holding a stick with a penis head. His phallus, we have seen, is not only the child's imaginary possession of power and potency but also the Flaming Wisdom that burns away the demons of ignorance and illusion and awakens the person to his real Buddha-nature. In its latter aspect, the phallus stands for a possible ideal state, the spiritual Beyond, the Lacanian Real. Here, religion uses the same materials that are found in the workshop of desire. The representations it crafts are often the transformed products of human desire. The phallic vajra, a symbol of what helps fulfil man's spiritual strivings, simultaneously also protects the child's sexual desire. The Thunderbolt is like an engine running on parallel tracks of desire and the spirit. Desire and spirit may never meet, but in our most creative and alive moments they tantalizingly brush against each other in the empty space that otherwise stretches between them.

Furthermore, it seems to me that the prelude to mystical enlightenment is the exhaustion of desire's performative repertoire. For most of us, the drawing of a curtain across the stage of desire only occurs with *dehanta*, the end of the body, our physical death. This is not true of the mystic who, while employing various spiritual practices to hasten the demise of desire's illusions and spectres, is also believed to be more porous to a lifelong pressure of the spiritual Beyond seeking to manifest itself across the border it shares with desire. An enlightened mystic generates—to use Bion's phrase in a different context—a 'beam of intense darkness'[21] which lights up the inner topography of the spiritual, a land not governed by the laws of the pleasure and reality principles. For a while at least, the spiritual Beyond floods the terrain of desire, submerging all its familiar, if often disquieting, features.

Desire and Spirit have a common home in the unconscious, moving in a psychic space (to use St Augustine's phrase) 'deeper than the deepest recesses of my heart' and 'higher than the highest I could reach'.[22] One reason why their cohabitation has not been more evident, why the unconscious is almost exclusively equated with desire, lies in the metaphors that have been used to characterize the unconscious mind. One of the horses which Plato's charioteer—the conscious, rational part of the mind—must control 'is a crooked great jumble of limbs . . . companion to wild boasts and indecency, he is shaggy around the ears—deaf as a post—and just barely yields to horse whip and goad combined'.[23] Freud, too, used the metaphor of the difficult to control horse, the id, that 'cauldron full of seething excitement', that dangerous basement of mental life which has its home in the unconscious. This tendency to equate the unconscious with the wild terrain of desire has not been limited to Western thought. The Buddha, too, compares the unconscious mind to a wild elephant that strays to 'wherever selfish desire or lust or pleasure would lead it'.[24] In Hindu thought, the counterpart of the unconscious mind is the *chitta*. Metaphorically, chitta is a monkey who, restless by nature, drinks wine and becomes even more restless. As if this were not enough, he is stung by a scorpion and (to complete the image of restlessness) a demon enters him.[25] Yet, in the Hindu scheme, chitta's restlessness is not its 'true' nature but one which comes into existence with birth and becomes ever more solidified in the course of human development. The real nature of the chitta is spiritual. In another metaphor, chitta is a lake with muddy and agitated waters which send up waves and thus hides the (spiritual) bottom which is visible only if the water is calm and the ripples have subsided. Desire's riveting performance has come to an end.

GANDHI AND THE ART OF
PRACTICAL SPIRITUALITY

$\mathcal{B}$etter known as the man who led India to independence from foreign rule and as 'father' of the nation, Gandhi is also a leading figure in the history of modern Indian spirituality. But can a psychoanalyst, trained to be suspicious of both saint and spirit, do justice to Gandhi's spirituality? Can he transcend the patrimony of his discipline, the hermeneutics of suspicion, and partake of Gandhi's greatness or communicate it to others without either idealizing it on one hand or reducing it to a matter of neurotic conflict on the other? I am determined to try, although Gandhi, with his lifelong struggle against his sexuality, obsessive ruminations around food and an overweening conscience that made him inordinately self-critical, does not make it easy for even the most sympathetic observer.

There have been other saints, St Augustine, for instance, who too have waged a war on their wants, but Gandhi is unique in leaving an exhaustive record, scattered over ninety-odd volumes of his writings, on his human failings and his determination to transcend them. It is his firm spiritual centre that holds together many of his inconsistencies and apparent contradictions: the wily politician and the saint, a socialist who is at times deeply conservative, an anarchist and a

traditionalist, a political and social activis
mystic, someone who is deeply religious ye
he could say he saw God even in the atheist's atheism.

Gandhi himself was supremely aware of his contradictions,
indeed of his inner conflicts. There is no mistaking it that he
is talking as much about himself as about Tolstoy when he
writes:

> The seeming contradictions in Tolstoy's life are no blot
> on him or sign of his failure. They signify the failure of
> the observer. Emerson has said that a foolish consistency
> is the hobgoblin of little minds. We would be utterly
> lost if we tried to live and show there was no
> contradiction in our lives. In trying to live in that
> manner, we would have to remember what we did
> yesterday and then harmonize our actions today with
> that; in trying to preserve such foolish harmony, we
> would have to resort to untruth. The best way is to
> follow the truth as one sees it at the moment. If we are
> progressing from day to day, why should we worry if
> others see contradictions in us. In truth, what looks
> like contradiction is not a contradiction, but progress.
> And so, what seems to be contradiction in Tolstoy's life
> is not really a contradiction, but only an illusion in our
> minds. Only the man himself knows how much he
> struggles in the depth of his heart or what victories he
> wins in the war between Rama [the ideal man] and
> Ravana [the demonical counter player of Rama]. The
> spectator certainly cannot know that. If the person slips
> ever so little, the world will think that there was nothing
> in him; this, of course, is for the best. One should not

condemn the world on that account and so the saints have said that we should rejoice when the world speaks ill of us, but tremble with fear when it praises us.[1]

Gandhi then goes on to give a rationale for his habit of publicly discussing his most private, inner conflicts and confessing to what many would consider minor lapses from the moral standards he had set for himself. In the same semi-autobiographical vein, he continues:

> When we become aware of the slightest lapse on our part or seem to have become guilty of untruth, intentionally or otherwise, we should feel as if we were burning, as if we were caught in flames. A snake bite or a scorpion sting is of little consequence; you will find many who can cure them. Is there anyone, however, who can cure the sting of untruth or violence? God alone can do that, and He will do it only if we strive in earnest. Hence, we should be vigilant against our weaknesses and magnify them to the utmost . . . If anyone pointed out a weakness in Tolstoy, though there could hardly be an occasion for anyone to do so for he was pitiless in his self-examination, he would magnify that weakness to fearful proportions . . .[2]

It is his spiritual self which the Mahatma—the 'great soul'—repeatedly tells us is the most vital and enduring part of him, one that involves the deepest layers of his being. 'It is an unbroken torture to me,' he writes in the conclusion of the introduction to his autobiography, 'that I am still so far from Him, who as I fully know, governs every breath of my life, and whose offspring I am.'[3] He tells us, 'My political work grew out of my spiritual preparation,' and, at another place, 'My Mahatmaship is worthless. It is due to my outward activities, due to my politics which is the least part of me and is therefore evanescent. What is of abiding worth is my insistence on truth, non-violence and *brahmacharya* which is the real part of me. That permanent part of me however small, is not to be despised. It is my all.'[4]

I will not go into the childhood antecedents of this spiritual self, something which has been done so well by my teacher Erik Erikson in his wonderful book *Gandhi's Truth*.[5] A towering figure in the history of our discipline, Erikson was firm in his belief that originology, the psychoanalytic habit of finding the causes of a man's whole development in his childhood conflicts, was as pernicious as a hagiographic teleology wherein ends are supposed to explain complex developments. To reduce a man of Gandhi's stature to early childhood traumas is both wrong in method and evil in influence, for it shuts out the possibility of man's partaking of Gandhi's message and person. To reduce great men to their traumas may prevent the excesses of idealization but it also forecloses a necessary admiration that opens us to them and to our best selves, to our ego ideals in the inelegant language of psychoanalysis. I will thus speak here as an unashamed admirer who nevertheless tries not to be blinded by impulses towards idealization.

What is this 'spiritual self' which is the prime mover of Gandhi's life? Gandhi variously called it the 'spirit' or 'truth' which he equated with God. 'I have always known God as Truth,' he writes to children in his ashram school.

There was a time when I doubted the existence of God, but even at that time I did not doubt the existence of Truth. This Truth is not a material quality but is pure consciousness. That alone holds the universe together. It is God because it rules the whole universe . . . For me this is almost a matter of direct experience. I say 'almost' because I have not seen face to face God Who is Truth. I have had only a glimpse of Him. But my faith is unshakeable.[6]

It was the Spirit, his 'inner voice' which, when the time came and he had prepared himself to listen, would dictate to him what he needed to do in any particular situation.

I do not claim to know definitely that all conscious thought and action on my part is directed by the Spirit. But on an examination of the greatest steps I have taken in my life, as also those that may be regarded as the least, I think it will not be improper to say that all of them were directed by the Spirit.[7]

For many secular persons—and I include myself in this company—the talk of Spirit arouses a sense of unease because of its strong religious connotations. The connection between the two is old. The ancient Greeks called this hidden aspect of man's nature, which led him to perform memorable deeds or create great works, *entheos*, the god within. And indeed in most religions, the manifestation of the Spirit in individual life is indistinguishable from God's will or divine revelation of one kind or the other. Indeed, Gandhi, too, on many occasions used religious terminology, describing his longed for spiritual state as being a state of communion with God, of surrender to His will and of being His instrument.

The religious appropriation of Spirit should not, however, lead the irreligious to reflexively reject the existence of this mysterious energy and the role it plays in human creativity. Saul Bellow, in his Nobel Prize acceptance speech, articulates the position of many of us who believe they have caught a glimpse of this hidden power that is not self-centred and which feels as if it emanates from somewhere else than the normal, everyday self with which we are so intimately familiar. 'The sense of our real powers, powers we seem to derive from the universe itself, also comes and goes . . . We are reluctant to talk about this because there is nothing we can prove, because our language is inadequate, and because few people are willing to risk talking about it. They would have to say that there is a spirit, and that is taboo.'[8] Even V. S. Naipaul, that most rationalist of writers who, for instance, values the conscious, thinking mind so much that he speaks of 'my detestation of music (widely regarded as potentially the most spiritual of art forms; Schopenhauer saw it as the manifestation of the noumenal)—the lowest art form, too accessible, capable of stirring people who think little,' admits that 'when the work is good I am not responsible'.[9] He tells his biographer that in such a phase, 'the material seemed to be given to him from nowhere' as he moved into that determined stupor out of which great books are written.[10] Mirza Ghalib, the great nineteenth-century Urdu poet, shares this sentiment when he says, 'My thoughts come to me / From somewhere Beyond / When Ghalib is attuned / To the music of the stars.'[11] Artists have called the spirit their Muse and there is a rare artist, whether agonistic or atheist, who does not believe in the existence of the Muse or does not have his own magical techniques of invoking and controlling it.[12]

Gandhi, an extraordinary artist of political and community life, arrived at his own methods of summoning the Muse, his famous 'inner voice', through a long series of experiments in self-cultivation and social action, some of which he describes in his autobiography, aptly titled *My Experiments with Truth*. His progress in seeking to align his life, personal and political, with his spiritual self was not linear. There were many setbacks and wrong turnings. The contact with the inner voice was often broken, especially at the end of his life, leaving him in a state of psychological depression and spiritual torment. Yet the whole process and the answers he arrived at through his experiments with 'Truth' are important for all of us, not as prescriptions to be blindly followed but as stimulants to find our own access to the whisperings of the inner voice and to rethink the role of the spiritual in collective life.

Gandhi's spiritual style is unique in so far as Gandhi outlined a vision of spiritual life that does not seek to renounce the world but to change it. Gandhi's spirituality is not set apart from the grime and tribulations of everyday life but informs it. He has given us a distinctive vision of how a person can pursue his spiritual destiny in a world rife with the ancient curses of injustice, exploitation, strife and violence. For those in political life, he showed that duplicity and aggressive scheming are not the only roads to success but that a politics of conscience, ruled not by Machiavelli but by regard for truth and fellow feeling, is eminently possible. For most of us, what I would call Gandhi's practical spirituality is more relevant to the leading of our lives than the spiritual seeking of contemplative saints meditating on the divine in their monasteries, hermitages or caves. Or, as Gandhi tells us, 'Throughout 35 years of unbroken experience of public service in several parts of the world, I have not yet understood that there is anything like spiritual or moral value apart from work and action.'[13] And, at another place, 'My spiritual seeking, whether or not original, has always been in the form of social service.'[14] It is Gandhi's practical spirituality, his vision of how we need to engage ourselves in our political and social worlds, that I want to look at more closely.

The core of practical spirituality is the development in the individual of what has been variously called empathy, fellow feeling, feeling of kinship with the whole of sentient existence and so on. 'Brotherhood,' Gandhi writes in one letter, 'is just now a distant aspiration. To me it is a test of true spirituality. All our prayers, fastings and observances are empty nothings so long as we do not feel a live kinship with all life.'[15] To one of his many critics, and there were many throughout his life and even after his death, who wrote to him suggesting that violence is the law of nature and that man is animal first and human afterwards, Gandhi replies that man can be classed as animal only so long as he *retains* his humanity and goes on to say:

> The correspondent apologizes for suggesting that I might regard myself as a remote cousin of the ape. The truth is that my ethics not only permit me to claim but require me to own kinship with not merely the ape but the horse and the sheep, the lion and the leopard, the snake and the scorpion . . . The hard ethics which rule my life, and I hold ought to rule that of every man and woman, impose this unilateral obligation upon us.[16]

For Gandhi, the development of kinship feeling is not sufficient by itself but involves a responsibility of translating it into action in everyday life as also in social and political action. In his public meetings, he often repeated the verse from St Matthew (vii.21): 'Not everyone that says unto me Lord, Lord, shall enter the Kingdom of Heaven but he who doeth the will of my Father who is in Heaven.' To Gandhi, the 'will of the Father' is the refusal to do harm, the 'not harming anyone in thought, word or action out of ill will or selfishness'.[17]

Gandhi's emphasis on altruistic action, which he regarded as the law of life in accordance with Divine will, has at its base the development of empathy as the supreme human virtue, an achievement higher than all other forms of human creativity, artistic or scientific. The development of this Einfühlung—the feeling into another—has, of course, many gradations but for Gandhi its epitome is the Upanishadic ideal of 'he who sees all beings in his own self and his own self in all beings'. Both altruism and empathy on which it is based have a troubled place in reigning currents of modern thought. Economic theory, based on the premise of Homo economicus acting rationally out of self-interest, selfishly, is as uneasy with altruistic behaviour as is sociobiology with its belief in the 'selfish gene' as essential to evolutionary success.

And what of my own discipline, psychoanalysis? Psychoanalysis is as much a product of modern West and the Enlightenment as the other disciplines. It, too, has been deeply suspicious of altruistic behaviour. Just as sociobiology allows a limited altruism in the animal kingdom—more in the sense of self-sacrifice that benefits the kin group rather than the empathy-driven human altruistic acts—psychoanalysis too exempts the 'proto-altruism' of materna caretaking[18] from its general view that altruism essentially rests on a pathological base. To be more exact, altruism, when it is not driven by psychotic delusions that lead to bizarre acts of self-sacrifice, is regarded as a subcategory of masochism. In psychoanalytic thought, altruistic behaviour in the individual is usually a defence against his strong aggressive strivings and envy, as also a superego-driven need to suffer and be a victim. Even in less conflicted cases, psychoanalysis tends to view altruism as the by-product of a 'healthy narcissism' which is essential for mental well-being, maintaining that a person can love others only if he first loves himself. For a psychoanalyst, a person acting on the Golden Rule, doing good, is nevertheless deriving a secret narcissistic satisfaction of being a do-gooder. But what if this dichotomy between narcissism and altruism is false? What if doing good to others is doing good to yourself?

Indeed, I would suggest that altruistic empathy and egotistic prudence are not in conflict but complementary to each other. Doing good to others is also doing good to yourself. Conflict-free altruistic behaviour raises self-esteem and thus contributes to the feeling of personal well-being. In other words, acting on the Golden Rule, present in various forms in all the world's religions, may be vital not only for an individual's spiritual progress but even for psychological happiness; it is not only a moral exhortation but an empirical fact.

Indeed, recent research in social neurosciences suggests that empathy, and altruistic behaviour that is motivated by empathy, may be wired into our brains. Witnessing the pain of a stranger activates a similar 'pain network' in our brains, although this empathy reaction almost disappears in men—in contrast to women—if the stranger is perceived to be a 'bad' person.[19] To witness good deeds—altruistic behaviour—gives rise to feelings of elation (some call them religious feelings) that are physiologically related to the rewarding release of the hormone oxytocin. In an ingenious experiment, the social psychologist Jonathan Haidt gathered forty-five nursing mothers with their infants in a psychological laboratory where half were shown videos depicting altruistic behaviour while the others watched comedy videos. Almost half the mothers who were shown the morally uplifting video showed increased milk flow or nursed their babies after watching the video while only very few mothers did so after watching the comedians. The first group also turned towards their babies more, touching them and clasping them to their breasts. Haidt comments that 'The effect was one of the biggest I ever saw.'[20] Other experiments demonstrate the presence of altruistic behaviour in children as young as eighteen months and even in two- to three-year-old chimpanzees who spontaneously help a familiar adult who appears in some distress.[21] Gandhi's contention, following the great *homini religiosi* of the world before him, on the primacy of empathic altruism in social life, the spiritual law he endeavoured to extend to the political world and which he believed is simplest to understand and the easiest to execute,[22] may indeed not be a utopian dream but an evolutionary reality. And as far as psychoanalysis is concerned, altruism should not be defined as a subcategory of masochism.

We have already talked of the essential presence of a wide-ranging empathy that must animate an altruistic act for it to be spiritual. Gandhi, for instance, does not believe that non-violence is limited to refraining from destroying life, a mere refusal to do harm. 'Non-violence means an ocean of compassion, it means shedding every trace of ill-will for others,' he says.[23] Non-violent or altruistic actions are not spiritual unless they have a vision of love behind them. Indeed, as the Catholic philosopher D.C. Schindler, commenting upon Pope Benedict XVI's recent encyclical *Deus caritas est,* writes, 'In its exaltation of the "other" simply because of his "otherness", there is a logic of hatred for the self hidden in the very structure of altruism. And if altruistic acts are founded in self-hatred, it is impossible that they give expression to truly fruitful generosity to others, no matter what immediate expression they might give.'[24] A truly, spiritually altruistic act can only be by a person who *loves* helping others, who is *personally* involved and gives the gift of his person along with whatever else he might give.[25] In their spiritual manifestation, there is no agape without eros and no eros without agape; love and generosity are inextricable.

On the larger political stage, where it cannot be expected that most people taking part in a non-violent protest have this vision of love, it is essential that at least the leaders directing the movement share it. Thus he regarded non-violent resistance—satyagraha or 'insistence on truth'—which he used with such success both against the Apartheid regime in South Africa and the British colonial rule in India, merely as an instrument. Depending on the degree of spiritual attainment and the empathic capacities of the user, it can be used both for mundane and for spiritual ends. Spiritually speaking, satyagraha is designed:

To reach the hearts of both the so-called 'terrorists'

[here he is talking about the Indian freedom fighters] and the rulers who seek to root out the 'terrorists' by emasculating a whole nation. But the indifferent civil resistance of many, grand as it has been in its results, has not touched the hearts of either the 'terrorists' or the rulers as a class. Unadulterated *satyagraha* must touch the hearts of both.[26]

(It is ironical, that September 11, 2006 was the 150th anniversary of the birth of satyagraha, in Johannesburg. September 11, 9/11, is now a date that has become inextricably associated with terror and violence.)

Gandhi was, of course, aware of the human limits to the practice of non-violence and the danger human narcissism poses to altruistic strivings.

I believe it impossible for one living in this body to observe non-violence to perfection. While this body endures, some degree of egotism is inescapable. We retain the body only so long as egotism persists. Bodily life, therefore, necessarily involves violence . . . The further we travel towards an ideal the further it recedes. As we advance in its search, we realize that we have one step after another to climb. No one can climb all the steps in one leap. This view does not imply cravenness of spirit or pessimism but certainly there is humility in it.[27]

Yet we must remember, and the social psychologist Roy Baumeister after reviewing the literature on violence and cruelty reminds us, that threats to self-esteem, narcissistic injuries, account for the largest portion of violence at the individual level. At a group level, it is moral idealism, an aspect of group narcissism that believes in the group's superior morality and mission, which is the main culprit.[28]

To look for guidance in counteracting the forces of narcissism, Gandhi turned to the Bhagavad Gita, one of the most revered texts of Hinduism. To Gandhi, the Gita's chief message is that since action, embracing all forms of mental and physical activity, is an inevitable corollary of life, spirituality cannot be disassociated from man's material life and worldly pursuits.[29] On the contrary, spirituality must inform daily life. In other words, a spiritual life has to be carved out of the field of human narcissism and its forces of greed, ambition and self-centredness. The way to do so, to overcome the insidious narcissism, is not to renounce action but to renounce the *fruits* of action. In other words, since actions are inevitable, the way to spiritualize the living of life is to become detached from the result of one's actions. Detachment does not mean indifference. Interpreting the relevant verses from the Gita, Gandhi says:

> In regard to every action, one must know the result that is expected to follow, the means thereto, and the capacity for it. He, who, being thus equipped, is without desire for the result and is yet wholly engrossed in the due fulfillment of the task before him is said to have renounced the fruits of his action.[30]

In more psychological language, Gandhi is suggesting that a passionate but non-narcissistic involvement in one's work is the path to spiritual progress and a spiritualization of life. And, for Gandhi, this acceptance of Gita's central message has as its corollary a way of life led in truth and non-violence: 'When there is no desire for fruit, there is no temptation for untruth or *himsa* (violence). Take any instance of untruth or violence, and it will be found that at its back was the desire to attain the cherished end.'[31] Detachment, the subjugation of Narcissus, does not come through knowledge but by what Gandhi variously called 'heart-churn' or 'heart-culture' in which an uncompromising ethical living of life is combined with deep introspection.

What does the seeker who has progressed far on Gandhi's spiritual path, who has come closer to Gandhi's ego-ideal, look like? There is, of course, a long list of qualities of such an 'enlightened' man, or the 'devotee' as Gandhi called him. Above all, he is fearless: 'Fearlessness is the first requisite of spirituality. Cowards can never be moral.'[32] The 'devotee' is indifferent to praise or censure, untouched by respect or disrespect, treats happiness and misery alike. Jealous of none, he is selfless, a fount of compassion, and so on. In his states of despair, and these were not infrequent, especially near the end of his life, Gandhi often lamented that he still had a long way to go to achieve this ideal. Yet, there were enough times when he lived the ideal, times full of energy, commitment and conviction that he was living in truth, following the 'truth as one sees it at the moment'.[33] These were the times when he heard his inner voice, on which he set great store, most clearly. The inner voice for Gandhi is the voice of the Spirit or of God—for Hindus they are synonymous—and Gandhi was stubborn in following its dictates even when they were contrary to the advice of all his friends or recommendations of his closest political associates. In fact, to hear the inner voice, sudden and unexpected, when one is in crisis and agonizing over which road to take, is a sign of being in a state of spiritual grace. It is the moment of truth.

Psychologists, loath to use a religiously tainted term such as the 'spirit', would say that Gandhi's decision about the direction he should take when he was in a state of ambiguity and much uncertainty came from his unconscious depths. Experiments show, they would say, that complex decisions are better left to unconscious processes. This does not mean that important decisions should be taken on impulse, without any thought. Our brain must have time to process all the relevant information and here, in the gathering of information, of facts and data, consciousness is superior to unconscious processes. It is only after a thorough and conscious collection of information has been done that the subsequent processes of reaching a decision should be left to the unconscious. The 'moment of truth', then, comes only to him who has lived with all aspects of a problem, the facts and figures, in such a way that he is always ready for a sudden synthesis.[34] Gandhi would prepare for this moment through fasting and in silent prayer for it was in the stillness of silence that his inner voice was at its most insistent. For others, the 'moment of truth' arrives in different settings. We are familiar with the many anecdotes about the unconscious solving of difficult scientific or artistic problems. Einstein, for instance, was very careful while shaving in the morning since ideas would suddenly come to him while he was thus engaged and he had to be careful not to cut himself with the razor. And a British physicist once told the well-known gestalt psychologist Wolfgang Koehler, 'We often talk of the three Bs, bus, bath and bed. That is where the big discoveries in our disciplines have been made.'[35]

Whereas artistic and scientific creativity is limited to

the individual, creativity in the social and political worlds, Gandhi's chosen field of action, required that the masses were ready to recognize *his* inner voice as their own. They would do so, Gandhi believed, if he was himself in a state of spiritual grace. He often used the simile of a rose:

> The rose does not need to write a book or deliver a sermon on the scent it sheds all around, nor on beauty which everyone who has eyes can see. Well, spiritual life is infinitely superior to the beautiful and fragrant rose, and I make bold to say that the moment there is a spiritual expression in life, the surroundings will readily respond . . . You cannot deal with millions in any other way.[36]

The consequence of Gandhi's stance is that any failure or setback in the community enterprise has one and only one cause: the spiritual shortcoming of the leader. He should be judged not by what he claims to be but by the progress of his followers on the path to non-violence and the ethical standards of the institutions the leader has sought to create. Gandhi states his credo of this total acceptance of responsibility clearly in writing about the ashram where he lived with a community that had gathered around him:

> The deficiencies of the Ashram reflect my own. I have told many people that they cannot know me by meeting me. When they meet me, I may even impress them as being good. Even if I am not good, people would believe I was because I am a lover of truth. My love of truth casts a momentary spell over people. In order to know

me, people should see the Ashram in my absence. There would be no error and no injustice to me in believing that all its deficiencies are a reflection of my own deficiencies. It is but true that I have drawn the crowd which has gathered in the Ashram. If, though living in the Ashram, they have not been able to overcome their weaknesses but have, on the contrary, developed more, the fault is not theirs but mine. The imperfection of my spiritual striving is responsible for this state of affairs.[37]

Each religious culture has sought to describe the obstacles in the path to spiritual progress. Buddhism, for instance, sees the elements of anxiety, greed, avarice and envy which form the cluster of grasping attachment as the chief affective obstacle. For Hinduism, it is the workings of the five passions: sexual desire, rage, greed, infatuation and egotism. To Gandhi, the greatest obstacle in his spiritual striving, the imperfection that stripped the rose of its fragrance and its beauty so that the surroundings did not respond, was the promptings of his sexuality. The manner in which he conceived the struggle and the weapons he chose to employ in a lifelong conflict with the god of desire have earned him the derision of many, especially in the West, who have discerned crankishness, if not worse, in his ideas that relate to sexuality. I have discussed this theme in detail—as well as the related ideas on food—elsewhere.[38] Here, I will only briefly mention the incident that has excited the most comment, both in India and in the West, although I tend to view it as one of the more poignant episodes in Gandhi's spiritual life, an occasion of compassion rather than moralistic prurience. I am, of course, talking of the eve of India's independence from colonial rule when large-scale violence between Hindus and Muslims had broken out in the eastern parts of the country. Whereas the other Indian leaders were busy in Delhi, preparing for the transfer of power, the seventy-seven-year-old Mahatma was trudging through the villages of Bengal and Bihar on a personal mission to restore peace between the two antagonistic communities. Gandhi was in considerable despair as he felt that people were no longer listening to him. The few close associates who accompanied him were helpless listeners to the anguished cries of 'Kya karun? Kya karun?' (What should I do? What should I do?) which they heard from his room in the middle of the night. He writes:

> I find myself in the midst of exaggeration and falsity. I am unable to discover the truth. There is terrible mutual distrust. Oldest friendships have snapped. Truth and Ahimsa [non-violence] by which I swear and which have to my knowledge sustained me for sixty years seem to fail to show the attributes I ascribed to them.[39]

For an explanation of his 'failure' to influence people and the course of events, Gandhi would characteristically probe for shortcomings in his sexual abstinence, seeking to determine whether Kama, the god of desire, had perhaps triumphed in some obscure recess of his mind, depriving him of his spiritual powers. 'Ever since my coming to Noakhali, I have been asking myself the question, "What is it that is choking the action of my ahimsa? Why does the spell not work? May it not be that I have temporized in the matter of brahmacharya?"' he replies to a close associate.[40] Thus in the middle of widespread political turmoil and religious frenzy, Gandhi wrote a series of five articles on celibacy in his weekly newspaper.

But more striking than this public evidence of his preoccupation were his private experiments wherein the aged Mahatma sought to reassure himself on the strength of his celibacy by having close women associates (his nineteen-year-old granddaughter among them) share his bed and then try to ascertain in the morning whether any trace of sexual feeling had been evoked, either in himself or in his companions. In spite of criticism by his co-workers, Gandhi stubbornly defended these experiments which he regarded as exercises in self-purification and tests of his celibacy and insisted that they be public even if they met general condemnation from his close associates.

> How can there be that self-purification when in my mind I entertain a thing which I dare not put openly into practice? Does one need anyone's approval or permission to do what one holds with all one's being to be one's duty? . . . It might disillusion millions who persist in regarding me as a Mahatma. I must confess, the prospect of being so debunked greatly pleases me. Thousands of Hindu and Muslim women come to me. They are like my own mother, sisters and daughters. But if an occasion should arise requiring me to share the bed with any of them I must not hesitate, if I am the *brahmachari* that I claim to be. If I shrink from the test, I write myself down as a coward and a fraud.[41]

Leaving aside the question whether these experiments were a self-testing or, in a period of despair, an old man's regression to an infantile need for motherly warmth, or both, I can only admire Gandhi's consistency in acting publicly on his convictions, however eccentric they might seem to the rest of the world.[42] But, then, he really did mean it when he said, 'Fearlessness is the first requisite of spirituality. Cowards can never be moral.'

In conclusion, let me say that besides the contemplative and ecstatic spiritual traditions, I regard Gandhi as a pioneer of a new spirituality. This is practical spirituality, a mode of being spiritually engaged with the world which may be uniquely suited to address the challenges of our times and the worlds still to come. With Gandhi as the model, we can say that in a state of spiritual grace the practical spiritual man combines sublime fearlessness with robust humour. He is filled with a serenity that comes from an unconcern with the consequences once the decision to act has been taken and painful choices faced. Above all, though, he is infused with a wide-ranging empathy that even extends to his opponents. Perhaps climbing the summit of love, loving one's enemy even when one is locked in a deadly struggle with him is only possible for saints. Most of us will consider ourselves fortunate if we can look up towards the peak from the base camp of an all-encompassing compassion. I will even be satisfied to reach the starting point of this spiritual expedition, namely a wide-ranging tolerance which the philosopher Ramachandra Gandhi, a grandson of the Mahatma, defined minimally as giving the benefit of doubt to others.[43]

EMPATHY IN PSYCHOANALYSIS
AND SPIRITUAL HEALING

$\mathcal{A}$t first glance, the spiritual practices of the main Eastern religions—Hinduism, Buddhism, Taoism—directed towards an 'absolute' rather than the phenomenal self of modern psychotherapy seem far removed from the concerns of psychoanalysis. If we except the Jungians, there is a venerable psychoanalytic tradition going back to Freud that tends to view religious or spiritual domains of experience as antithetical to psychoanalytic thought.[1] In spite of some respectful and non-reductionist treatment of religious–spiritual phenomena in the last quarter of the century, Freudian analysts have been often loath to acknowledge any similarities between the two.[2] Yet these spiritual practices—mainly forms of meditation—also have an implicit psychotherapeutic function in that the absolute self is said to be manifested through the phenomenal self which obscures and entangles the former in a web of distortions and illusions that need to be removed. Both psychoanalysis and the spiritual traditions acknowledge the primacy of the human mind in the production of suffering. They also accept that the mind can help in processing and containing disturbed thoughts and feelings that lead to emotional distress.

Thus in Hinduism, it is the workings of the five passions,

sexual desire, rage, greed, infatuation and egotism, which are held responsible for mental illness.

Similarly, Buddhists describe human suffering as due to causes internal to the individual mind: cognitive factors such as a perceptual cloudiness causing misperception of objects of awareness but also affective causes such as agitation and worry and the elements of anxiety, greed, avarice and envy which form the cluster of what the Buddhists call 'grasping attachment'.

Eastern spiritual traditions thus converge with psychoanalysis and psychodynamic therapies in the shared conviction that life does not happen to us but through us, and that it is false to believe that someone outside us is responsible for our distress.

Here, it should be made clear that the terms 'spiritual' and 'religious' are not identical. Religion and spirituality are not synonyms even if they are often regarded as such by many who have been brought up in the Judeo-Christian world view. The theological belief in God may be of great help in the striving for spiritual progress but it is not a necessity. In many Hindu, Buddhist and Taoist schools, an experiential understanding of the 'true' nature of the self is sought through an intensive practice of certain meditative–contemplative disciplines which do not require the presence of religious belief. In some early forms of Upanishadic and yogic mysticism, for example, there is no trace of love or yearning for communion with God which is considered the highest manifestation of spiritual mood in the Christian and Islamic mystical traditions (as also in the Hindu bhakti devotionalism), without which no spiritual illumination is conceivable. Zen Buddhist practice, too, is silent on the question of a Divine Being. In many Eastern traditions, then, spiritual progress is achieved entirely through the seeker's own efforts and without the intervention of divine grace.

Spiritual disciplines regard themselves as scientific in the sense that they describe the stages and processes of transformation of consciousness through specific practices. And, indeed, as we shall see later, their descriptions of mental states reached through spiritual, meditative practices are no longer solely dependent on the subjective but credible reports, through the ages, of advanced practitioners but have begun to gather tentative support from recent brain research in the emerging discipline of 'neurotheology' which seems to have identified the state of consciousness in advanced meditation through its traces in the brain: the quieting of parietal lobes and the lighting up of the frontal lobe during the intense concentration of meditation when all sensory inputs are blocked.[3]

At the outset, let me state that my focus here is not on a psychoanalytic understanding of meditative practices and psychic states reached by adepts of Eastern spiritual disciplines. The literature on this aspect is considerable, ranging from an emphasis on the (mostly earlier) characterization of these states as regressive in the pathological sense[4] to a more (mostly later) positive view of these states as integrative and adaptive.[5] My own thrust is more on the healing aspect of the interaction between the teacher-healer and the seeker-patient in the Eastern traditions and the contribution this understanding, including the self-understanding of the traditions, can make to psychoanalysis and the analyst–analysand interaction.

∽

In theory, Eastern spiritual traditions generally view their healing function, both of mind and of body, as incidental to and as a by-product of their main task: the purification of the mind, the removal of its distortions and illusions—its ignorance—in Buddhist terms. A purified mind is calm (or mindful) and thus a fit receptacle for the flow of a higher, transcendent consciousness. In most forms of yoga, for instance, the body, though important, is considered as subordinated to the mind. The gross body, our material sheath, is viewed as a shadow or creation of the subtle body we call the mind. The body is a mould into which the mind pours itself, a mould that has been prepared and can be changed by the mind.[6] Impurities of the mind not only lead to mental distress and illness but also, physically translated, manifest themselves in the body as disease. The removal of the cause—the impurities—also means the cessation of the effect: distress and disease. A purified mind makes for a pure body, a perfected mind for the perfection of the body. The perfection of the body, however, is not simultaneous with that of the mind but delayed till the impure precipitates of the mind, including karmic traces from past lives, have worked themselves out. This is a process which should not disturb the spiritual seeker although some may attempt to accelerate the purification of the body by certain forms of yoga, such as hatha yoga. Moreover, the spiritual disciplines are believed to be accompanied by profound alterations in brain physiology and chemistry, in the nervous system, in the digestive and secretive processes. These cannot be effected without some physical disturbances which, however, are temporary and never more than is necessary for the process.

In practice, of course, for most people, the attraction of a spiritual discipline, especially if a famous spiritual guide imparts it—the guru, rinpoche, *roshi* or any other kind of teacher—lies more in an expectation of immediate healing by the spiritual teacher than in an indeterminate promise of a purified mind and eventual spiritual perfection through meditation. Although there is a large variety of Eastern meditative practices, the differences between them perhaps insufficiently appreciated in psychoanalytic literature,[7] there is a much greater uniformity in the way the spiritual teacher is regarded across the Eastern traditions. The complete devotion and unquestioning faith expected of the seeker by the Hindu guru, for instance, is identical with the expectations entertained by the Tibetan Buddhist master, in spite of the differences in their respective yogic and Tantric meditation practices. In other words, the teacher more than the meditative discipline incorporates a therapeutic potential which draws to him many seeking relief from emotional distress or physical suffering.

This is certainly true of the devotees of well-known Indian gurus I have studied over the years.[8] The prominence of the healing offer is especially marked in the case of some contemporary gurus like Sathya Sai Baba, with a worldwide following numbering in tens of millions, who may fairly be described as the healer guru par excellence. An unusually large number of stories told about him by devotees are narratives of 'miraculous' healing. To a lesser extent, this is also true about spiritual guides whose healing offer is less conspicuous. In a study of Ma Anandamayi ('Mother of Bliss'), a famous female saint of North India with a large following, including the former Indian prime minister Indira Gandhi, eleven of forty-three interviews with her disciples contained incidents of her healing exploits.[9] Even in the case of an 'intellectual', modern guru like Jiddu Krishnamurti, with a following among the most modern and highly educated sections of society, it is not his teaching but the news about his miraculous cures that excited the greatest interest.[10]

Reading or listening to a number of healing stories, it becomes evident that the psychoanalytic theory which provides the most useful concepts in understanding therapy in the spiritual traditions is not the Freudian equation of cure with the patient's attainment of a mature genitality through his or her engagement with and a resolution of early Oedipal conflicts. Nor does the Kleinian goal of re-experiencing and ultimately overcoming the archaic layers of depression and paranoia do justice to cure in the Eastern traditions. This does not mean that the aspects of human experience highlighted by Freud or Klein are absent from the spiritual setting. In a long interaction with the guru, stretching over many years, a re-experiencing of early Oedipal conflicts and of archaic depression, suspicion and rage may indeed take place without being subjected to conscious insight except perhaps in a most fragmentary manner. What I wish to emphasize is that the theory of cure that makes the best *psychoanalytic* sense of spiritual healing is the self-psychology of Heinz Kohut.[11] According to this theory, analysis cures by restoring to the self the empathic responsiveness of the 'selfobject', of which the most important is the mother of infancy.[12] Of course, this does not mean that self-psychology shares the self-transcendental concerns of Eastern spiritual traditions. In its pronounced relational orientation, self-psychology is closer to Confucianism among the Eastern traditions rather than the more 'mystical' traditions of Hinduism, Buddhism and Taoism. Confucianism, too, conceives of the self in fundamentally relational terms. The self may begin with a physical individuality but expands along a web of related existences[13]—selfobjects—until theoretically it could identify with the whole universe. The Confucian tradition, though, does not seek the mystical perfection of the self's identification with the whole world but is content to recommend an ideal of mental health and psychological maturity where the self is appropriately responsive to and in tune with the situations and persons of daily life—family, friends, colleagues at work—without an artificial boundary that shrinks the existence of the self to that of an individual unit.

The disciples' accounts of healing interaction with the spiritual guide also make it evident that the seeker-patient's interactions with the teacher have the aim of establishing him as a highly reliable, always available selfobject for merging experiences. The teacher furthers this process by his willingness to let the seeker merge with what the latter perceives to be the teacher's greatness, strength, calmness, just as the mother once did when she lifted the anxious infant and held him against her body. Sai Baba constantly reminds his devotees that they are not separate from him; 'I am in you, outside you, in front of you, above you, below you. I am all the time around you, in your proximity,'[14] and 'Anything coming out of the depth of your heart reaches me. So never have any doubt on this account.'[15]

Teachers in many Eastern spiritual traditions have always known that a prolonged phase of meditation on the guru's face or form—practised, for instance, in the Guru Yoga of

Vajrayana Buddhism or in the Siddha Yoga of Kashmir Shaivism (a Hindu tradition), as also the contemplative uses of the guru's photograph in such modern sects as the Radhasoami Satsang and Sahaja Yoga—will contribute to and hasten the merging experience.[16] As a Siddha Yoga guru, Swami Muktananda, observes: 'The mind that always contemplates the guru eventually becomes the guru. Meditation on the guru's form, immerses the meditator in the state of the guru.'[17] As I have described elsewhere in a discussion of the Hindu guru as healer, other aspects of the guru–disciple interaction, such as the taking in of prasada (food offerings touched or tasted by the guru) or drinking water used to wash his feet, perform a similar function in the loosening of the seeker-patient's self boundaries and accelerate his experience of merging with the guru.[18] Gradually, the seeker-patient seems to acquire the capacity of summoning the guru's image with a hallucinatory intensity when in distress. Thus one patient, when lying sick with jaundice, feverish and in a state of drowsiness, reports, 'I do not know if I used to dream or it was reality. I always felt Baba constantly with me. He was caressing me, touching my hands. I never felt lonely. He was there all the time.'[19]

This access to archaic modes of contact in which a hallucinatory image of the guru is created to sustain a self in danger of losing its cohesion is reported by many seeker-patients and seems to be an integral part of the spiritual healing discourse.

With the spiritual healer's focus on a merger selfobject experience—in contrast to the analyst's effort to consolidate a sense of personal agency—the guru is initially much more active than the analyst in fostering the seeker-patient's idealization of his person. This is because of the signal importance most spiritual traditions attach to *surrender* as indispensable for mutative changes in the self, a surrender which can only be driven forward by intense forces of idealization.

Surrender of the self is, of course, also to be found in other religious traditions of the world. William James called it regeneration by relaxing and letting go. He characterized it as giving one's private convulsive self a rest and finding that a greater self is there.[20] The regenerative phenomenon which ensues on the abandonment of effort remains a fact of human nature.

He added, 'you see why self-surrender has been and always must be regarded as the vital turning point of religious life . . . One may say the whole development of Christianity in inwardness has consisted in little more than greater and greater emphasis attached to this crisis of self-surrender.'[21]

In Sufism, too, surrender to the master is a necessary prerequisite for the state of *fana fil-shaykh*, or annihilation of oneself in the master. Of the *iradah*, the relationship between the Sufi master and his disciple, the Sufi poet says, 'O heart, if thou wanted the Beloved to be happy with thee, then thou must do and say what he commands. If he says, "Weep blood!" do not ask "Why?"; if He says, "Die!" do not say "How is that fitting?"'[22]

Psychologically, surrender is the full flowering of the idealizing transference, with its strong need for the experience of merging into a good and powerful, wise and perfect selfobject—the guru. The seeker, in wanting to experience his self as part of the guru's self, hearing with the guru's ears, seeing with the guru's eyes, tasting with the guru's tongue, feeling with the guru's skin, may be said to be striving for some of the most archaic selfobject experiences.

∽

In interviews with seeker-patients, and in reading their accounts, what I found most striking about the healing encounter in the spiritual traditions is the seeker-patient's conviction of being profoundly understood by the guru.

In case after case, sometimes even in the first encounter, we hear reports of how the guru saw deep into the patient's heart, looked into the innermost recesses of her being, and the effect this understanding had on her. Mahamaya is a middle-aged Bengali woman who first met Sai Baba in 1992 and has remained a devoted follower ever since. She grew up in a middle-class household in Kolkata and remembers that both her parents had strong devotional and spiritual leanings. The outer shell of her biography—the events of her life: education, arranged marriage, children, part-time work as a teacher while her husband climbs the bureaucratic ladder in a state-owned insurance company—follows the conventions of an Indian middle-class success story.

There are, however, tantalizing hints of unhappiness in the marriage during its early years, some episodes of depression, especially one following the surgical removal of a malignant tumour in the kidney just before she met Sai Baba.

Mahamaya may be sparing in the narration of painful events of her life but not in the description of her emotional state prior to the first meeting with Swami (master):

I was steeped deep in crisis, and altogether shattered in body and mind. At that stage of my life, I was weak and had physically broken down, mentally in utter darkness. I was groping for true and abiding support.[23]

Visiting Baba's ashram together with her husband, she is sitting among a number of other visitors when Baba motions the couple to move to a smaller room adjoining the main hall for a private interview. Let me take the story forward in her own words:

As soon as my eyes met Swami's, He said, 'So you have come, with how much love I have called you.'

What a moment! A storm raged within me. I was stunned, dazed, and then broke down into a storm of tears. Since 1988, life had been a struggle for me beset with moments of trouble, mental agony, anguish, and depression overcoming me now and then. But never had I opened my heart to any one, not even my husband. God was the sole companion of my broken heart. An introvert from childhood, I had not even opened my heart to my parents. Something happened to me the moment I looked into the divine eyes, all restraint, and all constraints just vanished, tears welled up in my eyes and poured down my cheeks. I was sobbing like a child. I felt my heart was purified through and through.[24]

Baba then tells her that:

I should not worry about my son who, being busy with studies, was not writing letters. Secondly, I need not bother about my arthritis. In due course the pain would be reduced even though it would not go altogether. Thirdly, my younger daughter would have a safe delivery. These thoughts were in my mind no doubt but I had not uttered a word to him on these matters. He is the indweller. He knows all that goes on in our mind.[25]

Over the years Mahamaya's healing is evident in a marked increase in her zest for life and a creative outpouring in which she writes many poems and songs in Bengali and Hindi.

The patient's feeling of being deeply understood by the guru, of the Swami being the 'indweller'—of the guru's empathy, the analyst will say—is a primary feature of the healing discourse in Eastern, especially Hindu and Tantric Buddhist, spiritual traditions. I shall argue in the rest of this chapter that an exploration of the basic features of the spiritual guide's empathy can make a significant contribution to the psychoanalytic discussion of empathy.

ॐ

It seems to me that empathy, Freud's Einfühlung, the 'feeling into' another person, has been the object of a good deal of ambivalence in psychoanalytic literature, an ambivalence that has perhaps to do with what Freud, in a letter to Ferenczi, called its 'mystical character'.[26] The Oxford English Dictionary's definition of empathy seems unabashedly 'mystical' when it defines it as 'the power of projecting one's personality into (and so fully comprehending) the object of contemplation'. Although empathy constitutes the foundation of psychoanalytic work, of essence for gathering data for analytic interpretation, its connection to poorly understood unconscious processes in the analyst has surrounded the concept with a degree of unease in psychoanalytic discussion. Its general usage in psychoanalysis as one person's capacity to partake of the inner experience of another through unconscious attunement skims over the underlying mystery of the process. In other words, how does our normal non-empathic state, a state of self-experience with thoughts which are usually self-related,[27] change into a state where we can transcend the boundaries of the self to share the conscious and unconscious feelings and experiences of another self? Even the analyst's psychic state that is conducive to the operation of empathy, namely his evenly suspended, free-floating attention, when examined closely, seems to belong as much (if not more) to the meditative practices of spiritual traditions as to a 'scientific' psychoanalysis.

Consider, for instance, Freud's description of this psychic state:

> Experience soon showed that the attitude which the analytic physician could most advantageously adopt was to surrender himself to his own unconscious mental activity, in a state of evenly suspended attention, to avoid as far as possible reflection and the construction of conscious expectations, not to try to fix anything that he heard particularly in his memory, and by these means catch the drift of the patient's unconscious with his own unconscious.[28]

Ehrenzweig has called free-floating attention 'unconscious scanning', which depends on a conscious blankness and is liable to be disturbed by introspection.[29] Unconscious scanning clearly has a meditative character, very different from the process of introspection. Ehrenzweig compares unconscious scanning to Paul Klee's 'multidimensional attention' or to 'horizontal listening' in music where one hears polyphonic voices as opposed to normal, 'vertical' listening where one follows a single melody underscored by a harmonic background of accompanying voices. Horizontal hearing, in which several voices contending for exclusive attention cancel each other out, is totally blank in so far as conscious memory is concerned. This conscious blankness, however, does not preclude precision and fullness of information. In such comparisons and descriptions of (an ideal) free-floating attention, expert meditators will not fail to recognize advanced stages of meditative contemplation in certain Hindu and Buddhist spiritual disciplines. In other words, the analyst's potential for unconscious scanning or what Ogden calls the use of reverie experience, namely his unobtrusive thoughts, feelings, fantasies, ruminations, daydreams, bodily sensations and so on, seemingly unconnected to what the patient is saying at the moment,[30] may well be related to his capacity for metaphysical openness. It is this openness which bears on the analyst's capacity 'to feel the alive moments of an analytic session in a visceral way, to be able to hear that a word or a phrase has been used, has been made anew in an interesting, unexpected way'.[31]

The increasing psychoanalytic ambivalence towards the phenomenon of empathy seems to have its origins in Freud's changing views towards it as he aged. Paul Roazen, in his introduction to a paper by Hélène Deutsch, suggests that Freud took a far more distant and detached view of his patients in his later years than in an earlier, healthier period.[32] In his draft of 'Psychoanalysis and Telepathy' (1921), the 'secret essay' that was published posthumously in 1941, Freud had been sympathetic to the operation of such occult phenomenon as telepathy and thus, presumably, to the non-rational, intuitive, aspects of empathy. By 1927, though, he was taking a much more unambivalent stance on behalf of positivist science:

> The riddles of the universe reveal themselves only slowly to our investigation; there are many questions to which science today can give no answer. But scientific work is the only road which can lead us to a knowledge of reality outside ourselves. It is once again merely an illusion to expect anything from intuition and introspection; they can give us nothing but particulars about our own mental life, which are hard to interpret, never any information about the questions which religious doctrine finds it easy to answer.[33]

Not all his close followers shared Freud's criticism of intuition and introspection; Hélène Deutsch, for instance, viewed the analyst's intuition as a powerful therapeutic tool.[34] Yet with hardening attitudes towards the 'occult' in the wake of Freud's distancing from it, empathy too became an object of suspicion since there were no satisfactory criteria that distinguished it from telepathy in the analytic situation.[35]

In contemporary psychoanalysis, the unease with empathy is expressed variously. Many psychoanalytic contributions on the nature of empathy seek to temper its self-transcendental character by emphasizing that the analyst's identification with the patient is transient, non-regressive and under the analyst's ego control.[36] Beginning with Freud,[37] other analysts have emphasized the intellectual and rational aspects of empathy.[38] They have sought to domesticate its highly subjective, experiential character by enlarging the scope of the concept to include more neutral and cognitive aspects. Empathy, they assert, is not only an unconscious process in which the analyst shares the patient's experience for a short time but it also includes the placing of this experience in a larger, more objective and complex understanding of the patient and then responding with an appropriate interpretation.[39] The analyst's unconscious resonance with the patient oscillates with a more intellectual attitude,[40] to produce what has been called 'generative empathy',[41] 'vicarious introspection'[42] or 'emotional knowing'.[43]

Others, again going back to Freud who pointed out the difficulty of knowing whether or not our empathy is merely the projection of our own feelings on to the patient,[44] have surrounded empathy with danger signals.[45] What we often take for empathy may only be an 'empathic fantasy',[46] a 'projective distortion'.[47] Empathy is also imprecise in that the range of empathic immersion into another person can extend from a state of minimal feeling with him to the extreme of nearly becoming the other person and thus psychotic.[48] A prolonged identification with the patient is quite likely to be a pathological gratification of the analyst's own unconscious needs.[49]

The overwhelming majority of psychoanalytic contributions on the nature of empathy, then, have tried to distance it (perhaps also defensively) from its moorings in unconscious, still poorly understood but no longer completely mysterious mental states. These mental states, as we shall see later, seem to be quite similar to those traversed during the meditative process.

∽

In psychoanalysis, the analyst's understanding of the patient's inner state is primarily conveyed through a verbalizable and verbalized interpretation. In other words, the analyst's communication of empathy for the patient's inner state is primarily conveyed through words. Other means of communication, employing the aural, visual, tactile and olfactory senses, have received a limited attention in analytic literature[50] although analysts have long known that it is these other non-verbal means which constitute the fundamental layer of human communication in infancy.[51] To take the aural sense first, the *music* of healing, the prosodic aspects of the analyst's discourse—tone, accent, pauses, silences, intonation—may amplify or belie the empathy of his words. The importance of prosody differs with individuals but may also vary across cultures. In the major Eastern civilizations, for instance, the formal mode of communication required within the family and especially in hierarchical relationships, the reliance placed on prosody to divine the real meaning of a speaker's words, may be greater than in cultures which hold 'saying what one means' and 'meaning what one says' as highly desirable virtues.

The psychoanalytic setting, with the patient lying on the couch and an absence of eye contact between the patient and the analyst during the analytic hour, is actively inimical to the visual aspects—expression in eyes, gestures, facial mimicry, positions of body—of communicating empathy. The psychoanalytic emphasis on free association, fostered through a restriction of the visual channel, then has the disadvantage that it outlaws the *dance* of healing. And, of course, because of the rule of abstinence and the dread of 'crossing boundaries', amplified by psychoanalytic lore around the transgressions of once heroic and now tragic figures in the history of the discipline,[52] the tactile aspects of empathic communication between the analyst and the patient must perforce be completely excluded. Not for the analyst the clasping of a shoulder, the taking of a hand between one's own, the consoling stroke on the head, which convey empathic connection to a person as nothing else can in her periods of acute distress. For the analyst is acutely aware that a touch of understanding can soon become a caress of desire—or a stab of anxiety, a risk that spiritual teachers routinely take, sometimes with disastrous consequences for the seeker.

I must also add that like the experience of many people deprived of sight who develop acute aural or tactile perceptions, the emphasis on words in the analytic situation increases the patient's (and the analyst's) sensitivity to the nuances and particularities of language. At least this has been my own experience when in the full throes of transference during my training analysis in Germany, I not only began to dream in German but also to write fiction in that language, a gift that was snatched away when the analysis ended. This enhanced linguistic sensitivity receded when the transferential context which had made it possible disappeared.

Compared to the analyst, then, the spiritual teacher is relatively uninhibited (but also more endangered) in employing the full register of communication to convey his empathic understanding of the patient-seeker's internal state. In describing their experiences of the guru's empathy, patient-seekers in the Eastern traditions often emphasize factors other than the content of his words.

'I did not understand but I came away with the words alive within me' is a typical reaction.[53] The Indian spiritual traditions even have a technical term for the teacher's look, *darshanat*, 'through the guru's look', in which the seeker-patient is believed to be seen 'in every detail as in a clear mirror'.[54]

Like analysts, spiritual teachers, too, differ among themselves in their innate empathic capacities. Yet with their meditative practices designed to weaken what Brickman calls the encapsulation of the self,[55] not in an uncontrolled regression but in controlled decentring experiences, a spiritual discipline seems to open the doors to an empathic responsiveness that can extend to a high degree of identification with another person. Analysts, too, may have these 'transcendental' moments during an analytic hour. But these do not follow from being a part of a rigorous training explicitly designed to foster the mental state of what Bion called 'ignorance' and whose first stage is what Keats called 'negative capability', a passive, receptive state where there is no irritable reaching after fact and reason and no search for meaning.[56] For the nineteenth-century poet John Keats, it is the presence of the 'negative capability' that makes an empathic participation in the existence of other persons possible. The poet, perhaps a person of particularly strong empathic development, grasps the 'truth' about the animate and inanimate Other through this empathy and then reproduces it in literary images.[57] A radical increase in empathy for another person, claimed by spiritual adepts, is a part of their heightened responsiveness—empathy in its widest sense—towards the animate and inanimate worlds. In the *homini religiosi*, this empathy is also translated into a heightened metaphysical openness towards the Divine.

In their empathic identifications, analysts can perhaps never go as far as a few spiritual teachers are reputed to have done. In describing Anandamayi as a 'spiritually realized' person, for instance, a devotee explains: 'It means you have no personal center. The center of the realized person is everywhere. She can identify with whoever comes in contact with her. She becomes yourself and has your problems at the very moment and can help you from inside.'[58] Another disciple describes her as: 'She had no sense of "I" or "mine" and often simply mirrored the emotions of those around her; she seemed to have no desires of her own, so the incentives to her behavior took shape out of the wishes of her companions.'[59] Here Anandamayi approaches the ideal of the spiritual master met with in almost all Eastern traditions. In the Sufi tradition, for instance, the Shaykh's 'own bodily form has been annihilated and he has become a mirror; within it are reflected the faces of others . . . If you see an ugly face, that is you; and if you see Jesus and Mary, that is you. He is neither this nor that, he is plain; he has set your own reflection before you.'[60]

Compare these portraits of the 'enlightened' spiritual teacher with Keats's description of the identity—he called it Character—of the poet:

As to the poetic Character itself—it is not itself—it has no self—it is everything and nothing. It has no character—it enjoys light and hate; it loves in gusto, be it foul or fair, high or low—it has as much delight in conceiving an Iago as an Imogen. What shocks the virtuous philosopher, delights the chameleon Poet—A Poet is the most unpoetical of anything in existence; because he has no identity—Not one word I ever utter can be taken for granted as an opinion growing out of my identical nature—the identity of everyone begins to press upon me.[61]

The reflecting mirror ideal of the spiritual guru, then, is quite different from the earlier psychoanalytic ideal of the analyst as a blank screen; the analyst's self is hidden, unlike that of the spiritual master which often appears to be absent. Anandamayi, like some spiritual teachers, but unlike many analysts, can accompany the patient to the land of pre-psychological chaos met with in psychosis and borderline states. It is perhaps only Bion's ideal analyst who has eschewed memory and desire (and, in a later amendment, has also abandoned understanding)[62] who is a twin of the (also ideal) spiritual teacher.

Hindu spiritual traditions give detailed descriptions of the process that augments empathy to a point where there is no affective obstacle to an identification with another's experience. A complete empathic knowledge of another person, they claim, involves the activation of a normally dormant 'higher' faculty or consciousness. In yogic practice, for instance, reason, imagination, memory, thought, sensations have first to become sufficiently quiet for the higher faculty of Buddhi to become active and to know itself as separate and different from the lower qualities.[63] Buddhi is the yogic analogue of Bion's 'sense organ' of psychical qualities which responds to the broadcast of a 'sender' which dwells in the domain of the inner world and to which psychoanalysts need to develop a keener reception. Analysts, Bion maintained, needed to screen out the noise of sensible life so as to become more receptive to other messages from the psychical world.[64] This receptivity leads to expansion of preconscious communication channels and a greater capacity for retrieval from the depths of the psyche.[65]

In conclusion, one can say that, from a spiritual viewpoint, the chief obstacle to an analyst's empathy is his phenomenal, sensual self. Fuelled by the senses, the sensual self prevents the emergence of Buddhi. The meditative practices of the Eastern spiritual traditions are directed precisely towards the reduction of noise and glare produced by the sensual self. Thus although empathy is common to both spiritual healing and psychoanalytic cure, the concept itself veers towards its 'mystical' (in a non-pejorative sense) pole in the former case and towards its rational, intellectual pole in the latter. If we concede the spiritual teacher's claim, supported by personal testimony of spiritual adepts over the centuries, that the activation of Buddhi is accompanied by an extraordinary increase in his empathic capacity, then it follows that some kind of spiritual training may significantly enhance an analyst's potential for empathic identification. Such a training not only contributes to a greater ease with the setting aside of ego functions, making one less defensive against the anxiety of 'drowning', but can also expand the analyst's potential for 'reverie' or implicit listening, and thus for deep empathy.

Yet another way of increasing our empathic capacity may well be a constant and conscious practice of compassion till it becomes an ingrained way of approaching all living beings. To be consequent in one's practice of compassion is not an easy task. The Dalai Lama, who has been meditating for at least three hours every day for over fifty years tells this story about himself. In Dharamsala, where he lives, there are many mosquitoes. When the first mosquito alights on his bare arm, his thought is, 'Fine, my friend, you must also live. Have your meal of my blood.' With the second one, he is a bit irritated. When the third one comes buzzing to the dining table, he squashes it flat. The Buddhists believe that your thoughts when you are dying have a huge effect on how you are reincarnated in your next birth, pure, spiritual thoughts ensuring a higher form of consciousness in the next life. 'When I am dying,' Dalai Lama says with his trademark smile, 'I will make sure that my bed is covered with a mosquito net.'[66]

For psychotherapists, then, the augmentation of their empathic capacity is of signal importance. This is true even if one does not regard empathy as a primary curative agent as Kohut does, but is prepared to concede that it is indeed a very significant tool for gathering data in the treatment situation. After all, even the most sophisticated interpretation in psychoanalysis can only be as good as the data on which it is based. Empathy, and the meditative state that underlies it, may well be the sluice through which the spiritual enters the consulting room and where it flows together with the art and science of psychoanalysis in the practice of psychotherapy. This is not to suggest that psychoanalysis should lose its distinctive character by an indiscriminate borrowing from Eastern spiritual traditions. Psychoanalysis itself can be viewed as a singularly modern meditative praxis, unique in its emphasis on being a meditation that is joint rather than individual. Yet in the spirit of Freud's legacy of openness to other disciplines (Freud recommended the study of anthropology, folklore and mythology to the budding analyst), analysts need to remain open to the possibility that an Eastern meditative discipline, such as the Buddhist Compassionate Meditation, could become a part of their training if, as claimed by its practitioners, it demonstrably contributed to an enhancement in empathic capability. The traditional Freudian suspicion of the spiritual domain, and the cultural pride in psychoanalysis as a uniquely valuable product of Western civilization and imagination, should not come in the way of such borrowings.

THE USES OF RITUAL

The preferred data for a psychoanalyst from which he seeks to derive insights that may contain the potential for further generalization are his case histories. And the case history I am going to use in trying to understand the uses of a ritual is my own. My understanding of ritual, then, is inextricable from my own experiential background which I will try to articulate although I am acutely aware that all such articulations are fated to remain incomplete.

My childhood memories of rituals derive from the house of my grandparents, a dark, three-storied house in a narrow lane off a main bazaar of Lahore, a house with little space but much warmth, which was the site of many ritual festivities. The rituals were celebrated within a typical Indian extended family, a sprawling collection of my father's dozen brothers, sisters, cousins and assorted uncles and aunts on visits that in some cases could extend over a year. My childhood memory of rituals is of gaiety and excitement interspersed with solemn interludes. I have a vague recollection of ritual specialists, the pandits and pujaris, who presided over some of the religious rituals, and a much more vivid memory of the kitchen, full of women, that was in action from early morning till night, a source of steaming hot delicacies coming out of deep-bottomed frying pans.

My memory of rituals is also inseparable from the stories around them, stories told by one aunt or another as I drifted off to sleep at night, fighting my tiredness all the way. The stories, narrating the origins of a ritual and warning against misfortunes in store for those who neglected its proper performance, were legends from the epics but also folk tales about princes and princesses, and magicians who turned them into birds and animals and back again into people. My earliest association with a ritual, then, is of a time outside the reality of everyday life, a time of excitement and enchantment, an experience suffused with a warm glow, filled with light even if not with Enlightenment.

It was my father who introduced (Western) Enlightenment into my experience of rituals. My father was an uncompromising rationalist who looked down upon religious rituals as superstitious relics of bygone eras of which modern man was well rid. A civil servant by profession, my father was the first of his family to immigrate from a bazaar into the Indo-Anglian world of the Raj, the world of Civil Lines and army cantonments, of clubs and picnics. Temperamentally incapable of being moved by religion or the beauty of Indian ritual, art or music, and with a strong belief in rationality as the desirable principle of ordering human affairs, he readily identified with his British superiors whom he saw as valiant fighters against the decay of an Indian society riddled with magic and superstition.

My father was also a gentle, considerate man who never objected to my mother's temple visits or interfered with her rituals, although we were all aware of the distaste with which he regarded these activities. The only rituals he acknowledged as being of some value were those marking the major transitions of life: birth, marriage and death. These, he said, were valuable not because of their worthless religious content but because they made us pause before the enduring mysteries of human existence.

My own stance towards ritual, as one can easily comprehend, was ambivalent. I loved participating in the ritual life of my grandparents' house. Even in our small nuclear family, I loved helping my mother in her preparations for Diwali or Rakhi. I enjoyed the measured unfolding of a familiar sequence of actions, the coming together of people one loved and was loved by, the solemnity of the occasion which soon gave way to gaiety and abandon, the feeling of being pulled out of ordinary life into a magical space where time had stopped—all of which were greatly seductive to the young child. Yet, on the other hand, like any other boy I could not wait to become a grown-up man and felt impelled to adopt the attitude towards ritual of the adult I admired most—my father.

My father's attitude towards ritual was reinforced by my beginnings as a psychoanalyst. Psychoanalysis is rightly called the hermeneutics of suspicion and Freud was indeed, in the words of the philosopher Paul Ricouer, a 'master of suspicion'.[1] In relation to ritual, psychoanalysis naturally refuses to accept the religious explanation of ritual which, for me, is enshrined in the stories I heard as a child. A classical, Freudian analyst, then, is not interested in what a particular ritual reveals but in what it conceals; in other words his intellectual excitement will lie in ferreting out the unconscious content the ritual is defending against. The fact that in this enterprise psychoanalysts can and sometimes do 'go over the top', coming up with fanciful explanations that strain every nerve of credulity, is seen as an acceptable risk of the analytic enterprise.

As a budding analyst, I learnt that when psychoanalysts talk about ritual they do not mean it in the way scholars of religion and anthropologists sometimes do: a ceremonial form that deepens the individual's connection—with nature, community and the sacred—and from which the individual emerges purified and with a sense of awe and significance. For them, ritual means the actions of a person suffering from an obsessive–compulsive disorder, someone who is subject to a panic attack if he deviates even the slightest bit from a rigid routine. He or she may be someone who, for instance, is enslaved to the hand-washing ritual, scrubbing his hands raw in a tortured solitude, yet never feels that they are ever clean. I would not, however, summarily dismiss the psychoanalytic view of religious ritual as originally obsessional in intent simply out of hand. The preoccupation with creating an order out of a threatening chaos, which is the hallmark of the obsessional, is also reflected in theories of the anthropologist Mary Douglas and the scholar of religions Roy Rapaport which, too, stress the ordering function of ritual.[2] Analysis may be revealing to ritual merely its caricature. Yet it is a revelation that is important in making us aware of the ever-present possibility and danger of a ritual resembling its distorted double.

As a child, then, ritual was an amalgam of superstition, mystery and exhilaration, and as a young adult in psychoanalytic training it carried connotations of mental illness. Even at that time I sensed, though, that psychoanalysis was leading me away from my native Indian imagination— full of myths and marvels, many of them around ritual activity and performance—into an iconoclastic way of seeing the world where, if one looked hard and deep enough, all gods have clay feet. It is only now, as I get older, that even as I continue to keep faith with Freud's suspicious vision, I become less and less enamoured of the bargain I made when I was young. Perhaps it is true that the innocent eye sees nothing. On the other hand, the view of the suspicious eye remains partial.

My father's attitude towards ritual is not difficult to understand. I have said he was an old-fashioned rationalist although the adjective 'old-fashioned' for someone who considered rationality synonymous with modernity would have certainly annoyed him. He was very much a Macaulayian product who idealized the modern West—that is, the confident, imperial West of the first half of the twentieth century—and had swallowed one of its myths, that the core of a ritual is rigid precision. As a young man, he had been influenced by the reformist Arya Samaj movement which, in turn, had incorporated the Puritan belief that ritual is mere empty form without true religious content, that rituals are only husks or empty shells. Times have changed. His modernism has given way to a postmodernism (with its own myths) and to pervasive doubts in what had been his certainties. Over the years, as a layman rather than a scholar of rituals, I have come to appreciate the uses of ritual and have moved to an intellectual position that is far removed from that of my father. Yet remnants of his stance towards ritual are stuck in my own psyche, like a food particle lodged between teeth, constantly explored by an uncomfortable tongue. Today, I can appreciate the significance of rituals in human life yet at the same time I cannot help but suspect ritual specialists—less the scholars than the professionals—of a nostalgic conservatism, of championing faded or dead rituals that have little relevance for the world we live in. I can be an enthusiastic participant in the celebration of rituals but have also developed fine antenna for rituals that are truly empty, where the letter has triumphed over spirit. In fact, even as a participant in a ritual activity, I am sometimes so busy operating my own private radar, scanning for signs of a fake, routinized performance, that I may easily miss the central import of a particular ritual. It is as if I want to confirm my father's views on ritual at the same time as I want to refute them.

Now, of course, there is a vast variety of rituals. There are the rituals of daily life, for instance, the family ritual of coming together for a meal. And then there are the once in a lifetime ceremonies around major life events that sponsor our transition from one cultural status to the other. There are healing rituals and academic rituals, political and judicial rituals, rituals of war and rituals of peace, rituals of sport and rituals of science, and so on. I am not a taxonomist by temperament and will not seek or dwell upon criteria for their classification but come to the main theme of this essay: the psychological uses of ritual. Now there is a widespread agreement among scholars in ritual studies that rituals are important for the formation of identity on cultural, social and personal levels. Psychologically speaking, the value of a ritual lies in the degree to which it contributes to strengthening a person's sense of identity. This contribution can be to the individual aspect of personal identity, for instance, in rituals that encourage us to look at and lend significance to our life cycle by emphasizing its beginning, transitions, end, as also its connection to nature and the cosmos. Or the strengthening may be of the group aspect of personal identity through rituals that accent our connection to others who belong to our family, caste, creed, tribe, nation and so on. These teach us our group's sanctioned ways of doing things, heightening the sense of 'us' while at the same time excluding outsiders, 'them', who do not know the right way. Another psychological classification can be between those rituals that defend or protect our sense of identity against a perceived danger by closing the psyche, and others that augment personal identity by opening the psyche to novel experiences. In my personal mythology, I like to think of the former as 'father rituals' while the latter are 'mother rituals'. The protective, conservative rituals can, of course, degenerate into rigid compulsions such as the persistent hand washing while the enhancing, transformative rituals are in danger of slipping into a delusional grandiosity. In a somewhat more theoretical aside, what I am highlighting here is a vexing problem of ritual studies, namely the uniting of the conservative and transformative functions of ritual activity.

When I look back at my own erratic engagement with rituals, the rituals that were most vital, that made me feel most alive, combined *both* these qualities in a psychologically energizing moment. In other words, these were rituals that closed certain threatening experiences of psychic danger while they simultaneously opened the psyche to experiences that produced a distinct sense of self which is difficult to put into words but is approximately captured by such terms as 'wonderment', 'enchantment', 'awe' or 'a sense of the sublime'.

Here, I will give only two illustrations of rituals where the two aspects that appear contradictory, in fact, turn out to be complementary, where the closing and opening of experience are not mutually exclusive but combined. Let me begin with a quiet ritual that is familiar to most of us, either from our memories of being a child or from our adult life as a parent, or both.

It is night. The four-year-old boy is in his bed but not yet asleep. He is waiting for his mother to put him to bed. The household is becoming quieter, preparing to see off yet another day. The mother comes in and sits down on the bed, in her usual place where they can look at each other while she tells him a bedtime story. From her sigh of contentment as she squats down cross-legged on the bed, folding her feet under her, the boy senses that she is more relaxed today, that as she begins the story which he has heard many times before, her engagement with him is less coerced by duty and is more an expression of a free choice. She *wants* to be with him, just the two of them. For her, the bedtime ritual is also a safe haven from the demands and tensions of the large family. She takes obvious pleasure in repeating those familiar step-by-step actions that will lead to his falling asleep. In the beginning, he sometimes interrupts her narration, correcting her when she makes a mistake, reminding her of an omission, but slowly the ambience of the bedroom changes. An invisible net of safety descends around the bed, cocooning mother and child in its folds even as night obliterates the familiar landmarks of the day. The sounds outside the house, the barking of stray dogs, the whistle of the engine as the night train to Delhi pulls out of the train station, seem to come from far away. Occasionally, the mother's hand caresses his hair as her storytelling voice washes over him, arming him against the approaching blanking of consciousness. He is no longer afraid of the free rein sleep will give to the approaching unknown and its possible terrors. As they look at each other in a mutual affirmation, his mother's face glowing with an inner light as it bends over his, the child not only senses an absence of fear in the room but a presence of something extraordinary yet utterly familiar, an enchantment that suffuses the last moments of his waking consciousness. Later, as an adult, he will find a name for these remarkable moments of the bedtime ritual. They were, he would now say, marked by the presence of what the psychologist William James called the *numinous*, a magical quality which, at bedtime every night, transformed his mortal mother into a hallowed and beneficent divinity.

My second example is a much louder one. It is of a ritual performance involving possession and healing. These rituals can take place in healing spaces such as temples and dargahs especially known for this purpose or they can be characteristic forms of worship, such as the possession dance and drama in south-western India where male ritual specialists dress as and become possessed by the spirit of fierce goddesses during temple festivals. These rituals, like all others, certainly lend themselves to psychological interpretation. Indeed, I too have interpreted some of the healing rituals in a North Indian temple and in the Oraon tribals of Jharkhand in an earlier work.[3]

Here, though, my focus is not on psychological interpretation of either the content or context of a ritual but on what makes a ritual come alive. I want to emphasize the experience of rituals rather than their explanation. Or, to be more exact, I would like to give precedence to the interpretation of experience rather than of content. The rituals I have talked of above are infinitely more dramatic than the storytelling ritual of bedtime. They are often in the form of a polyphonic play, with voices of the shaman or the exorcist, of possessing spirits or deities, of the patient, speaking singly or in a cacophonic bedlam. These are voices that are raised in anger, that can threaten, shout, plead. The purely healing ritual may be accompanied by a great deal of movement: rhythmic swaying of the upper half of the patient's body or a violent sideways shaking of the head, unexpected dancing movements of the patient or the shaman, beatings that are self-administered or are the province of the healer, and so on. In the temple festival rituals of Kerala, as described by Sarah Caldwell, ritual specialists enact the mythic deeds of the goddess in a possession trance, providing devotees with a direct experience of the goddess in living form.[4] Speaking from my own experience, I can testify that such a ritual, with its embodied deities or spirits from another world, can produce a mild state of altered consciousness in even the most sceptic of onlookers. The dramatic aspect of these healing and worship rituals is certainly one reason why they can shake an onlooker's habitual way of experiencing the world, give ordinary reality a significance it did not have earlier, even when he *knows* that what he is witnessing is just a 'drama', a performance.

Being part of an audience in such rituals is another reason for the mildly altered feeling of consciousness, essentially the feeling that one's normal psychological defences and controls have been weakened and one's sense of identity has become shaky. In other words, one is more open to influences, both threatening and beneficial. Or, if you will, to use another vocabulary, there is a feeling of vulnerability to both malignant and helpful spirits, to protective and fierce deities. The touch and press of other bodies is only one of the stimuli that hammer at the sense of individual identity with an intent to weakening it. Other excitations, channelled through vision, hearing and smell are as much involved in this assault as are the more subliminal exchanges of body heat, muscle tension and body rhythms that take place when one is part of a large group or crowd. The weakening of identity goes hand in hand with a relaxation of controls over impulses and emotions and a gradual abandonment of critical faculties and rational thought processes; in short, there is a regression to mental states of early life. In this highly receptive and, yes, also expectant state, I have often felt the menace of the patient's possessing spirits even while being aware that the menace is a projection of my own internal state, the surfacing of my own 'evil' from unconscious depths as my defences are relaxed. And then, as the ritual proceeds further, the threats recede. What comes to the fore is the vision of a deeply beneficent universe to whose care any disturbances of body or mind have been entrusted. Once again, as in the bedtime ritual of the child, we encounter those magical moments which bring these rituals to pulsating life. These are moments that can take birth only if the mind senses and closes to a situation of psychic danger while simultaneously opening up to unknown but beneficent forces.

Rituals for me, then, at least the ones I consider 'alive' and psychologically the most valuable, are not symbolic of something else. They are not gateways to other worlds or doors to other realities. They are not stimulants to 'deeper spiritual appetites' but, along with poetry, music and art, they are all we have to satisfy these appetites. We have called the arresting, transformative moments of rituals magical, and that is what a truly alive ritual does: it conveys the experience of magic, of enchantment—nothing more, nothing less. One can say about a ritual what the great jazz musician Duke Ellington wanted to convey about the soul of jazz when he titled one of his songs 'It don't mean a thing, if it ain't got that swing'. The peril a ritual transforms is as illusory as the safety it conjures. A ritual is an illusion, yes, but a necessary and even desirable illusion that lights up the narrow, mundane world of daily existence, a world which has always been 'inadequate to our experience and unequal to bear the burden of our hopes'. For a brief period of time, it lets us transcend what the Irish poet William Buler Yeats called 'the desolation of reality'.[5] Yet, however much I, and modern people, may long for that early stage of life where the magic of ritual was taken for granted, I also know that a return to ritual experience characterized by the childish naiveté of idealized, simple and literal forms is impossible. Perhaps all one can aspire to in relation to ritual is what Paul Ricouer suggested a believer could achieve in relation to his religious faith: a 'second naiveté',[6] a sophisticated, adult, reflective affirmation of ritual that never lets go of a necessary, corrective suspicion.

RELIGION AND PSYCHE:
READING FREUD'S 'THE FUTURE OF AN ILLUSION' IN GOA

I first read 'The Future of an Illusion' when I was eighteen.[1] A youth who had grown up in provincial Indian towns, I had come to study mechanical engineering in Ahmedabad, a large city intimately associated with Gandhi and the Indian freedom struggle. It was here that I came across Freud's writings and took my first steps into the world of Western ideas and imagination. I cannot pretend that I understood everything I consumed so voraciously. I sensed, though, that in my inner world I was being gently guided away from my native Hindu-Indian imagination, full of myths and marvels, infused with a romantic longing, into an iconoclastic way of seeing the world where, if one looked hard and deep enough, all gods have clay feet. The experience was exhilarating.

'The Future of an Illusion' was an important text in my personal 'freedom struggle', also because its appraisal of religion neatly dovetailed with the assessment of my other youthful passion which, too, held emancipatory promise: Marxism. Freud is pure Marx when he talks of civilization being imposed on a resisting majority by a minority which understood how to obtain possession of the means to power and coercion (p.6) or when he talks of the economic basis of civilization, with its problems in acquisition and distribution of wealth, before discussing civilization's 'mental assets' or 'psychical inventory' of which religion is such an important part in reconciling men to their lot.

For someone who grew up at a time of Indian history in which Western modernity—a catch-all term for political democracy, scientific rationalism and philosophical individualism—was idealized by many as the most desirable future for our society, Freud's attack on all religion, including my Hindu heritage, was as welcome as the similar Marxian dismissal of religion as the opiate of the masses. For many of us, intoxicated with the ideas of Western gurus, political freedom from colonialism had not yet translated into freedom from a colonized consciousness.

Decades later, no longer resonating to Nietzsche's call that every past is worth condemning,[2] questioning my earlier idealizations of Western civilization and the Judeo-Christian tradition of which psychoanalysis, in spite of some differences in its image of man, is an integral part, I come back to Freud with some of the scepticism of the great sceptic himself.

Rereading 'The Future of an Illusion' at a later stage of life and self-consciously as a member of a non-Western cultural group, I am struck by how much of Freud's analysis of religion is inseparable from 'personal factors in his own experience' and 'subjective expectations' (p.5) from his cultural–historical background. As a Hindu (or one who has wittingly donned the Hindu robe for the purpose of this essay, though not without some playful effort), I am not surprised. It is a tenet of Hindu philosophy that an individual 'action' can only be understood in the context of the culture of his country (*desha*), the historical era in which he lives (*kala*), the efforts required of him at his particular stage of life (*shrama*) and, lastly, on his innate psychobiological traits (*guna*). An individual can never know the configuration of all these factors, his experiential background, in any absolute sense. This basic Hindu postulate is similar to the argument advanced by the philosopher Charles Taylor that our experiential background can never be articulated in a complete way 'since any articulation supposes a background, making a total explication incoherent'.[3]

If one replaces the Hindu doctrine of guna which, in line with belief in rebirth, considers human development to be anchored in a succession of previous lives, with its Freudian counterpart, that is, guna being grounded in infancy, in our 'prehistory', rather than a previous birth, the traditional Hindu emphasis on the relativity of all human action, including the production of knowledge, is surprisingly modern. Its emphasis on relativity, though still rare in psychoanalytic writings,[4] coincides with influential currents in modern Western philosophy which, too, at least highlight the desha–kala, the cultural–historical, embeddedness of human knowledge and understanding.[5] And although psychoanalysis, both clinical and theoretical, often challenges some cultural–historical verities of its era—Freud's writings are an outstanding example—culture and history, desha and kala, operating silently in the background of our awareness, inevitably compel psychoanalysis to be *more* an artefact of its times than its critic.[6]

Let me take an example from the beginning of 'The Future of an Illusion' where Freud sounds very much like a conservative, patrician Brahmin viewing the lower castes when he writes of the need for leaders of a superior quality:

It is just as impossible to do without control of the mass by a minority as it is to dispense with coercion in the work of civilization. For masses are lazy and unintelligent; they have no love for instinctual renunciation, and they are not to be convinced by argument of its inevitability; and the individuals composing them support one another in giving free rein to their indiscipline.'[7]

Here, using the four Hindu 'coordinates' of action, the desha and kala of Freud's observation are fairly obvious: Europe between two world wars when extremist ideologues of the left and right were creating mass movements imbued with messianic fervour. Building on the classical notion of masses described by Gustave Le Bon (whose own ideas, in turn, were framed by the dread the French upper classes felt in relation to the revolutionary masses), Freud's reflections on mass psychology are coloured by the ideological concerns of the time, namely the liberal fear of loss of individual autonomy in a collectivity and the socialist concern with how to make the desired collectivities more tolerable and tolerant. Moreover, Freud's strong anti-religious stance has also been related to the tradition of radical rationalism in which he had grown up[8] as also to the cultural context of Freud's Vienna in which a conservative Catholic Church encouraged anti-Semitic policies that were finally to culminate in Nazism.[9]

The *individual* coordinates of 'The Future of an Illusion', its shrama–guna components, are more elusive. At a pinch, one can relate Freud's dismissal of religion as universal obsessional neurosis of humanity to his specific *ashrama* or stage of life, with its illness and deepening pessimism, especially when we know that at other stages of life his views were relatively more benign. In his introduction to Oscar Pfister's correspondence with Freud, Paul Roazen reminds us that a decade earlier, in his case history of the Wolf Man, Freud is much more appreciative of religion than in his consistently negative comments in 'The Future of an Illusion'.[10] And as for the guna, personality traits arising from his 'prehistory', that went into Freud's lack of musicality towards religion, it has been suggested that it had to do with his need to repress any fear of maternal hostility which was then transferred on to father and religion.[11]

∽

From viewing 'The Future of an Illusion' through a traditional Hindu methodological lens, let me go to a Hindu view of its vastly more important content. Here, I will only take up Freud's discussion on the psychological origin of the idea of God and the nature of illusion, which appear strange, if not incomprehensible, to a thoughtful Hindu who is otherwise in sympathy with Freud's project of a psychological deconstruction of religious ideas. 'Eighty years after you wrote "The Future of an Illusion", I wonder if you would still adhere to its main conclusions,' our imaginary Hindu (following the literary conceit often used by Freud) would begin. 'I know that you called it "childish" almost immediately after you wrote it[12] and that later, in "Civilization and Its Discontents" you somewhat softened your severe stance by saying you were not talking about deepest sources of religion but with what a common man understands by his religion.[13] Yet in all your writings on religion you do not retreat from two main conclusions: the idea of God as an exalted father and the illusory nature of the religious belief system, "so patently infantile, so foreign to reality".[14] I will thus respond to these two ideas without speculating on how you would have revised them, something you never hesitated to do in the light of new observations and evidence. A major difficulty I have with "The Future of Illusion" is your emphasis on religious ideas and beliefs that make up the religion of the "common man". In Hinduism, though, ritual and practice take precedence over belief which is taken much less seriously than is the case with the so-called Abrahamic or Semitic religions of Judaism, Christianity and Islam. A Hindu may believe in one God or many gods or be an atheist, but what makes him a Hindu are his ritual practices and adherence to rules than to doctrines. Ritual is prior to theological doctrine, historically and conceptually,[15] and Hindu religious identity does not depend on shared ideas and beliefs but on rituals relating to rites of passage, worship at home or temple (puja), festivals and pilgrimages. In short, a Hindu is as a Hindu *does*.'

Hinduism's ideas of God have been shaped by many cross-currents throughout its 5000-year-old history. Over the centuries, the interaction and synthesis of these currents of belief have resulted in contemporary Hinduism with its varied teachings and diverse cults. The Indologist Axel Michaels writes:

> Belief in stones and trees having souls (Animism, Pantheism) exists side by side with the belief in higher gods, the monotheistic worship of one god is as much possible as the polytheistic or demonical adoration of many gods, demons and spirits.

The religion is lived through ritualistic (Brahminism, Tantrism), devotional (Bhakti), spiritual-mystic (asceticism, Yoga, meditation) and heroic forms . . . And yet to a large extent all these forms are peacefully practiced besides each other. One can almost say that religious post-modernism has been realized in India: 'Anything goes.'[16]

It is thus difficult to have a definitive Hindu view of any religious idea, including that of God. One can speak of one god or many gods while acknowledging that there are schools which, like Buddhism, ignore the existence of god altogether. In some early Upanishadic and yogic mysticism, for instance, that date back to 600 BCE, and are considered by some as the signature forms of Hindu religiosity, there is no trace of love or yearning for communion with God which is considered the highest manifestation of spiritual mood in the Christian and Islamic mystical traditions.

Freud links the 'birth of God' to two motives: one manifest and the other deep. The manifest motive is to defend against the superior, crushing forces of nature by humanizing them and by relating to them in an infantile way: 'We can apply the same methods against these violent supermen outside that we employ in our own society; we can try to adjure them, to appease them, and, by so influencing them, we may rob them of a part of their power.'[17] Freud's formulation of the manifest motive applies to the origins of ancient Hindu pantheon. Most Vedic (c.1500 BCE) gods, though not all, are nature gods and goddesses who can be appeased by offerings and worship, asked for help or, as in the case of the wrathful Rudra, persuaded not to interfere with the human world.

Today, the nature gods are rarely worshipped although they are present in ancient invocations that accompany some of the religious rituals. This manifest motive for the birth of God is not a matter of dispute for a thoughtful Hindu. What he will respectfully contest is the validity of Freud's deeper motive, the universality of a father-complex—the fear of the father combined with the admiration and longing for him—that goes into the development of the idea of God.

'You are much more circumspect at the beginning of your inquiry into religion when, aware of the historical and cultural relativity of your arguments, you restrict them to present-day white Christian civilization,' our imaginary interlocutor will continue. 'But as soon as you come to the deeper motive that conflates father and God, you observe no such limits, for instance, when you assert that "the primal father was the original image of God, the model on which later generations have shaped the figure of God" (p.42) or when you call religion the universal obsessional neurosis of humanity which, "like the obsessional neurosis of children, arose out of the Oedipus complex, out of the relation to father" (p.43). Your whole construction of the idea of God arising from the constellation of the helpless child and the protective father who is also a source of danger, an ambivalence you claim is deeply imprinted in every religion, seems to be absent or at least insignificant in Hindu religious imagination; at best, it is but a minor theme in a grand symphony.'

Indeed, iconographically, the only god who is represented with a grey beard and who may be equated with a protective father today, the Creator Brahma, is a forgotten and neglected god who has but only one temple in India dedicated to his worship. In the three main Hindu traditions, Vaishnavism, Shaivism and Shaktism, related respectively to the worship of Vishnu, Shiva and the many forms of the Great Goddess Maha Devi, it would be difficult if not impossible to locate the father in a Hindu's worshipped deity. This is not a question of monotheism versus pantheism, since most Hindus believe in the existence of a one Almighty although at the same time they feel free to worship it in different forms. In the *Brihadaranyaka Upanishad* (c. 900 BCE), the sage Vidagdha asks another sage, Yajnavalkya, How many gods are there? Three thousand and three, and three hundred and three, Yajnavalkya replies. But as Vidagdha keeps on repeating the question the number of gods keeps on reducing: thirty-six, six, three, two, one and a half and, finally, one.[18]

'If we just talk of the protective function that you ascribe to a father-god,' Freud's Hindu opponent continues, 'then in Hindu iconography this function is parental rather than fatherly. Whether in temples or coloured lithographs so easily available in India's bazaars, Hindu gods are generally not depicted alone but have their consorts by their sides. Very often, a deity is not invoked on its own but as part of a couple: Sitarama and not Sita and Rama, Radhakrishna and not Radha and Krishna. In the two main Hindu traditions of Vaishnavism and Shaivism, the feeling of helplessness and the looking for protection from God seem to be the last thing on a devotee's mind. Take Krishna, a form of Vishnu and one of the most popular gods: in Krishna's iconography and in his representation in religious poetry and song, he is either a toddler—with the child's attributes of freedom, spontaneity and delight in self, which Hindus consider as divine attributes[19]—or an eternal youth with either his lover Radha at his side or playing the Divine Flute in the middle of a dancing circle of young women.

'In Shaivism, the god Shiva, originally the Destroyer of the Hindu trinity (Brahma is the Creator and Vishnu the Preserver), could have conceivably resembled the father-god of Judeo-Christian and Islamic religious traditions. But, Shiva, above all, is the untamed god who cannot be reduced to any single function. He is the Lord of the ascetics but also the indefatigable lover whose sexual embrace with his consort Parvati lasts thousands of years. As Hari-Hara, he is half Vishnu and half Shiva; as the androgyne Ardhanarishwara, he is the "Lord who is half woman", Shiva and Parvati at the same time. Today, Shiva is not thought of as wrathful Deity charged with the periodic destruction of Creation, but as Shankara ("dispeller of doubt or difficulty") or Shambhu ("benevolent"), that is, a friendly, sweet god, occasionally prone to excess.'

If it is ambivalence in relation to father that is a deep motive in the construction of God, in Hinduism we have to look for this ambivalence in relation to the mother and to the Goddess, a motive that is upfront in the Shakta tradition. The innumerable village goddesses, all regarded as manifestations or aspects of the Great Goddess, Maha Devi, are earthy, mundane, attuned to the uncertainties and troubles, the desires and prayers of daily life.[20] In comparison, the male gods are remote. The Great Goddess is an ambivalent figure, both the furious, bloodthirsty Kali with a lolling tongue and the gentle, benevolent Parvati with breasts overflowing with maternal milk. It is these ferocious and protective forms—the poet-scholar A.K. Ramanujan calls them 'goddesses of tooth' and 'goddesses of breast'[21]—that are combined in the Great Goddess, in the primal mother, so to speak, rather than in the primal father, which underlies the idea of Divine in the Shakta tradition.

'I believe that the mainstream attitude towards God in the three Semitic religions has misled you to generalize it to other religions of humankind,' our imaginary Hindu says to Freud. 'In devotional practice, besides the surrender, obedience or filial love, which are the normal ways of approaching a father-god, Hindus seek to establish an intimacy with the Deity through other *bhava*s ("moods" or "emotions") that are congruent with the personality of the believer; in the Hindu world one size does not fit many. Some of the other attitudes towards God, for instance, are *sakhya*, the emotion of friendship, *madhurya*, the romantic and erotic feeling, or *vatsalya*, the feeling of a mother towards her child: in other words, God as friend, lover or child. The latter attitude towards the Divine, prominent in worship of child Krishna, completely reverses the father–child accent you have placed on man's relationship to God. Indeed, feelings of awe in relation to God, and the degrees of fear associated with awe are rare in the Vaishnava or Shaiva traditions; awe distances and separates rather than binds and joins.'22

With the advantage of hindsight, the 'thoughtful Hindu' will say that Freud's ensnarement in the desha–kala web, in the 'archaeology of knowledge'23 or the systems of discourse that shackle what can be thought and expressed at a particular historical juncture, is nowhere more evident than in his blanket dismissal of illusion. For all his creativity, Freud was an heir to the European Christian world where illusion had long implied trickery and deception, a world where Satan was the arch-deceiver. Whereas in an earlier era, illusion was demonical, the logos of science replacing that of theology in Freud's time led him to call it pathological. Religion is not only analogous to obsessional restrictions but was made up of wishful illusions 'such as we find in an isolated form nowhere else but in amentia, in a state of blissful hallucinatory confusion'.[24]

'Hindus are much more positively inclined towards illusion,' enter Freud's imaginary opponent. 'They tend to associate illusion with playfulness, or even benevolent deception rather than with malignancy. If you ask an orthodox Hindu about the nature of the world or why it was created, the answer would be, "It is God's play—*lila*." This is illustrated in myths and metaphors which are typically Hindu ways of viewing the world. A myth of child Krishna (an incarnation of Vishnu) and his mother Yashoda conveys some of this quality Hindus associate with illusion.

'One day, Krishna's playmates reported to his mother that her son had been secretly eating mud. Yashoda scolded the child who protested his innocence. Mother, he said, if you don't believe me you may look into my mouth. When the mother of God did so, she saw the whole universe in the little mouth. Motionless space, the four directions, the earth with its mountains, islands and oceans, wind, fire, the Milky Way with moon and stars, water, sky, gods, the five elements of potential matter, the three qualities of creation, all were in Lord Krishna's mouth; and in it she saw her own village and herself. Yashoda was confused. Is this a dream or illusion made by God? Or is it a delusion of my own mind? Seeing his mother disturbed, Krishna closed his mouth. As soon as he did so, the vision was erased from Yashoda's memory and, once more in the grip of the maternal illusion, he was again her little boy.'[25]

In Vedic thought, *maya*, generally translated as illusion, is identified as a particular power of the gods to create, a power later ascribed to magicians, artists and, in certain Indian philosophies, to each one of us, at every moment of our lives.[26] In psychoanalysis, this equation of illusion with creativity is associated with the influential work of Donald Winnicott[27] which accorded 'permission' to many later analysts to view the role of illusion in religion in a non-pejorative and indeed positive light.[28] Winnicott would have shaken his head at Freud's anecdote about one of his children's matter-of-factness in which Freud admires the child turning away every time in disdain from the narration of a fairy tale when told it was not true.[29]

It is not as if Hindus completely deny the dark side of illusion. The negative quality associated with maya has not been absent in Hindu philosophical thought or popular imagination. Based on the important work of the Indologist Wendy Doniger (with its delightful title, *Dreams, Illusions and Other Realities*), the Hindu doctrines of illusion and the way these have influenced the attitudes of the average Hindu can be summarized as follows:

The Vedic concept of maya as a kind of artistic, creative power gradually led to its reinterpretation. In later Hinduism, maya is ambivalent. On the one hand, maya stands for the creative potential of gods, the divine play (lila) and, on the other hand, for magic, illusion and deceit. In both cases, though, maya can best be translated as 'transformation'.[30]

In other words, some Indian philosophies regard maya mostly as a positive fact of life, to be embraced, while others will agree with Freud's evaluation and regard it as negative, to be combated. Both attitudes towards illusion coexist in the Hindu mind. But how do Hindus draw a line between illusion and reality? Don't Hindus dismiss the whole of existence, the empirical world of our senses, as maya, as illusion? This commonly held view of what a Hindu believes is the nature of our world is misleading. There have been indeed extreme idealist Hindu philosophers (but more Buddhist ones) who gave an ontological status to the omnipotence of imagination. The ideas of these philosophers, Nagarjuna, Vasubandhu and others, find strong echoes in the contemporary ideas of such psychoanalysts as Matte-Blanco, who imply that imagination is the basis of reality.[31] Of course, an average Hindu does not really believe that 'We are such stuff as dreams are made on.'[32] In other words, for a Hindu to say 'that the universe is an illusion (*maya*) is not to say that it is unreal; it is to say, instead, that it is not what it seems to be, that it is something constantly being *made*. *Maya* not only deceives people about the things they think they know; more basically, it limits their knowledge to things that are epistemologically and ontologically second-rate.'[33]

What Hindu theories about the 'softness' of reality do is dissolve the very hard and fast line between illusion and reality that Freud makes in 'The Future of an Illusion'. For a Hindu, there are many different kinds of reality: of concrete experience, mystical visions, memories, dreams. Some are more real than others. As Doniger further remarks:

These [realities] would have to be set out at various points on a spectrum that has no ends at all. A comparable, though different range of perceived realities exists in the West, but the traditional Western way has been to assign each phenomenon to one or other of the basic polar oppositions of hard and soft, real and unreal. This India refuses to do.[34]

Even Karl Popper, the most empirical minded of modern philosophers who may be expected to sympathize with Freud's views on illusion and reality, is more flexible on this question:

Realism is essential to common sense. Common sense, or enlightened common sense, distinguishes between appearance and reality . . . But common sense also realizes that appearances (say, a reflection in a looking glass) have a sort of reality; in other words, that there can be a surface reality—that is, an appearance—and a depth reality. Moreover, there are many sort of real things.[35]

❦

If Freud's imaginary opponent is wondering how the Master would have reacted to the Hindu take on 'The Future of an Illusion', I believe I can reassure him. Freud was certainly not dogmatic. We know he was ever willing to change his views in the light of new evidence and was often a harsh critic of his own work, especially when it ventured out of the clinical into the cultural domain. 'If experience should show—not to me, but to others after me, who think as I do—that we have been mistaken,' he writes, 'we will give up our expectations.'[36] 'The Future of an Illusion' is not necessarily a mistake but contains partial truths that cannot be universalized. From a Hindu perspective, its major deficiency lies in its basic premise: the importance Freud attaches to religious beliefs and ideas in his portrayal of religious man. Hinduism, though not indifferent to this aspect of religion, certainly considers it much less relevant than religious *experience*, whether in ritual, religious celebration, pilgrimage, or in mystical experience. For a Hindu, it is the arresting, transformative moments in religious practice that constitute the core of religion. Perhaps Freud the novelist—'In my mind I always construct novels'[37]—and the artist—'I am really by nature an artist . . . My books in fact more resemble works of imagination than treatises on pathology'[38]—rather than the positivist scientist of 'The Future of an Illusion', would have agreed.

And what of the young man at the beginning of this essay who had once welcomed 'The Future of an Illusion' as an indispensable ally in his struggle to jettison the romantic 'illusions' of his native Indian imagination and to move from the realm of *mythos* into that of *logos*? Older now, he continues to keep faith with Freud's ironic vision of human existence although he is much less enamoured of the bargain he made when he was young.

AFTERWORD: SPIRIT AND PSYCHE

At the end, to describe the relationship between the spirit and the psyche, I must take recourse to metaphor that comprehends body, psyche and spirit as intimately related entities with fuzzy boundaries that flow into each other. I envision the psyche as a large lake. The waters of this lake are warm, heated by the energy of sexuality, aggression and, above all, narcissism, that comes pouring in from the surrounding earth, the body, and keeps the waters in turbulence, ripples that can become waves which may assume frightening proportions. At the bottom of the lake, there flows the cool stream of the spirit, its water fed by the subterranean spring of connection, loving connection, which is kept apart from the upper layers by the difference in temperature between the two. Spiritual adepts dive often and deep into this stream, although there is perhaps none among them who does not also normally dwell in the shallower reaches of the lake, sharing the joys, sorrows and circumstances of our common humanity.

But we, too, ordinary mortals, are not cut off from the spiritual stream. Given the turmoil of life, the cool water often surges up to the surface in trickles though rarely in flood. These are perceptible moments of elation in the presence of nature, the thrill in front of a work of art, the ineffable intimacy with the beloved after the sexual embrace when the bodies have separated and are lying together side by side, but are not yet two in their responses. There are many other such moments, minor epiphanies, which escape our conscious awareness since we expect the spiritual to be an exception rather than a rule in human life.

The spiritual quest, except for those rare people who have set their sights on the summits of spirituality, is then not a search but a *re-cognition* of the many instances when the spirit touches the psyche. The touch may be barely noticeable, like the wing of a butterfly whispering against the cheek. The quest is not to catch and hold the butterfly which will die and become desiccated if captured. The challenge is to be aware of the spiritual moments as we travel through life, to look around and see again with the innocent eye. There is a story about the Zen monk who had been meditating for many years in a cave. When he became old and felt the approach of death, he expressed his desire to finally visit the fabled valley of flowers of which he had heard so much when he was a child. 'It is beyond that yonder range of mountains,' he was told. The monk started climbing, his gaze fixed on the mountain peaks. When he reached the top of the range, he asked another monk going in the opposite direction how far the valley of flowers still was. 'Look behind you,' he was told. When he looked back, the monk found he had walked through the valley of flowers without seeing it.

An invaluable ally for 'seeing' is imagination which the romantics have always considered as the basis of reality. Kant held imagination to be the basis for all productive knowledge. Einstein agreed when he asserted that 'I am enough of an artist to draw freely upon my imagination. Imagination is more important than knowledge. Knowledge is limited. Imagination encircles the world.'[1] We usually think of imagination as the ability to make images, although the capacity to access and elaborate on early memories is equally important. Indeed, it is a complex and often a playful combination of the two which characterizes a bold leap of the imagination. As we now know, the area of the brain activated in remembering the past and visualizing the future is the same in both cases.

Imagination, which in the words of the psychoanalyst Gilbert Rose 'propels one beyond prosaic reasonableness into a less tangible world of emotions, dreams, suggestions, and impressions where there is no rigid separation between self and not-self',[2] is not opposed but complementary to reason as the capacity to think clearly. Even Keats, that most eloquent partisan of imagination, visualized as an ideal a smoothly working partnership between the two, holding that a truly complex mind would be 'one that is imaginative and at the same time careful of its fruits' and would exist 'partly on sensations and partly on thought'.[3] The enemy of imagination is not reason but its overbearing, overcritical form that disparages the illogical and the incongruent, smothers spontaneity and feeling, banishes the poetical, excludes all tendencies towards symbol and metaphor, and acknowledges the primacy of only the statistical and the quantifiable. If the pathological form of imagination is delusion, that of reason is obsession.[4]

Keats, however, went beyond the psychology of imagination—the use of condensation, displacement, symbolism—into its spiritual dimension by highlighting the imaginative process as a union between the knower and the known. In his 'unitive' imagination, 'No sooner am I alone than shapes of epic greatness are stationed around me' and 'according to my state of mind I am with Achilles shouting in the trenches, or with Theocritus in the Vales of Sicily'.[5] Gustave Flaubert, while writing *Madame Bovary*, confides to a friend:

> It is a delicious thing to write, to be no longer yourself but to move in an entire universe of your own creating. Today, for instance, as a man and woman, both lover and mistress, I rode into a forest of an autumn afternoon under the yellow leaves, and I was also the horses, the leaves, the wind, the words my people uttered, even the red sun that made them close their love-drowned eyes.[6]

I would call the spiritual dimension of imagination *connective* rather than unitive, with the latter constituting an end point of a spectrum, accessible only to individuals with extraordinary spiritual gifts. Just as an altruistic act is spiritual only if it is informed by a vision of love, imagination is spiritual only when it is connective. Connective imagination is not only limited to literary works and creation of images in painting and sculpture but is the essence of many religious forms. I am especially thinking of Tibetan-Buddhist and Hindu Tantra which have the visualization of the deities and the devotee's union with these mind-created forms as their central spiritual practice. Here, let me mention only one of the many Tantric techniques, *nyasa*, in which a Tantrik visualizes the goddess and then introjects her into the various parts of his body by touching them. The imaginative world created by the Tantrik is not the personal one of the artist (or the psychotic) but is both shared and public in that it is based upon, guided and formed by the symbolic, iconic network of his religious culture. Another example of religious practice where connective imagination manifests itself is in the daily ritual puja of an orthodox Hindu who gets the gods to dwell in the various limbs and parts of his body before he begins to chant his prayers. Indeed, a great attraction of religious practices may well lie in the opportunity they afford the believer to release and exercise his capacity for connective imagination.

Connective imagination, then, is not only the basis of much great art and some visions of science and philosophy but is also the underlying principle of many religious rituals and spiritual disciplines. Perhaps the time has come that connective imagination also receives serious attention in psychological disciplines concerned with the apprehension of the world and, in its form as empathy, as a singular mode of understanding other human beings, assumes its rightful place at the head of the psychotherapy table.

NOTES AND REFERENCES

Introduction

1. The terms 'romantic' and 'rational' are used descriptively, without attaching a value judgement.
2. See R. Schafer, 'The Psychoanalytic Vision of Reality', *International Journal of Psychoanalysis*, **51**, 1970, 279–97.
3. See D. Klugman, 'Empathy's Romantic Dialectic', *Psychoanalytic Psychology*, **18**, 2001, 684–704.
4. China, because of its Confucian tradition, was anyway never as romantic as, say, India.
5. C. Lindholm, *Culture and Authenticity*, Malden, MA: Blackwell, 2008, 141–42.
6. In a talk at the conference on 'Emerging Images of Humanity', Fetzer Institute and Eranos Foundation, Ascona, 5–11 August 2007, the religious scholar Ursula King called it 'the global quest for spiritualities'.
7. Lindholm, op. cit. In Western art, of course, the romantic impulse did not weaken as much as in other areas of life. Metaphysical questions maintained their significance for artists from Wassily Kandinsky to Francis Bacon, from Joseph Beuys to Damien Hirst. To touch, 'refine and enrich' the 'soul', the 'spirit', has become a central concern for many artists today who believe that the ability to summon

a vision of the divine without sentimentality is one of the highest skills of the artistic profession.

Childhood of a Spiritually Incorrect Guru: Osho

1. The literature on the Rajneesh movement is vast. It includes accounts by his followers or those who broke with him, as also by scholars of sociology and new religious movements. In the latter category see especially, Hugh B. Urban, 'Zorba the Buddha: Capitalism, Charisma and the Cult of Shree Rajneesh', *Religion*, 26, 1991, 161–82; Lewis F. Carter, 'The New Renunciates of the Rajneesh Shree Rajneesh: Observations and Identification of Problems of Interpreting New Religious Movements', *Journal for the Scientific Study of Religion*, 26(2), 1987, 148–72; C. Lindholm, 'Charisma and Consciousness: The Case of the Rajneeshee', *Ethos*, 30(3), 2003, 1–19.

2. For the remarks on Gandhi see, for instance, G. Feuerstein, *Holy Madness: The Shock Tactics and Tactical Teachings of Crazy Wise Adepts, Holy Fools and Rascal Gurus,* New York: Paragon House, 1991, 26; for the remarks on Mother-Teresa see, B. Mullan, *Life as Laughter,* London: Routledge and Kegan Paul, 1983, 25.

3. Ma Amrit Chinmayo, *Sex: Quotations from Rajneesh,* Shree Rajneesh Foundation, Woodland Hills, CA: Lear Enterprises, 1981, 52.

4. cit. in Urban, 170.

5. cit. in Mullan, 43.

6. Dalai Lama in the 'Workshop on Buddhism' held in New Delhi, 21–23 December 2006.

7. One of Rajneesh's close female disciples describes her experience of Dynamic Meditation: 'Dancing wildly, carried along by the pulsating rhythm of the music and the energy of Rajneesh's presence, the top of my head suddenly exploded

with the most powerful orgasm I had ever experienced. It flooded every recess of my body; I fell to the ground, people dancing over me and around me. I was stepped on, kicked; it didn't seem to matter. I was "off" somewhere. Ecstatic, in bliss.' cf. S.B. Franklin, *The Promise of Paradise*, New York: Station Hill Press, 1992, 52.

8. Lindholm, op. cit., 19–20.
9. Rajneesh, *Glimpses of a Golden Childhood*, Rajneeshpuram, OR: Rajneesh Foundation International, 1985, 664.
10. Rajneesh, *Books I Have Loved*, Rajneeshpuram, OR: Rajneesh Foundation International, 1985, 175.
11. *Glimpses*, 74–75.
12. Franklin, op. cit., 279, 325; H. Milne, *Rajneesh: The God That Failed*, New York: St. Martin's Press, 1987, 186.
13. W. James, 1902, *The Varieties of Religious Experience*, New York: Touchstone, 1997, 37.
14. Swami Devgeet in his introduction to *Glimpses*, no page number.
15. As the psychoanalyst and theorist of narcissism Heinz Kohut has shown, for someone with an 'ego of average endowment' the delusional claims of a grandiose self can be highly disruptive. In a person of superior gifts, though, it is precisely this grandiosity that fuels their ambition and pushes them to outstanding achievement. See H. Kohut, *The Analysis of the Self*, New York: International Universities Press, 1971, 108–09.
16. Rajneesh, *Glimpses*, 15–18.
17. Ibid., 77.
18. Ibid., 45.
19. Osho (Rajneesh), *Autobiography of a Spiritually Incorrect Mystic*, New York: St. Martin's Press, 2000, 20.
20. *Glimpses*, 106.
21. F. Nietzsche, *Beyond Good and Evil*, H. Zimmern (tr.), White Field, MT: Kessinger Publishing, 2004, Aphor. 58.

22. *Glimpses*, 8.
23. G. Moraitis, 'The Ghost in the Biographer's Machine', in J.A. Winer and J.W. Anderson (eds), *Psychoanalysis and History*, Hillsdale, NJ: Analytic Press, 2003, 105.
24. *Glimpses*, 20.
25. Ibid., 8.
26. Ibid., 11–12.
27. Osho, *Autobiography*, 20.
28. *Glimpses*, 60.
29. Osho, *Autobiography*, 6.
30. *Glimpses*, 37.
31. *Autobiography*, 9.
32. *Glimpses*, 52.
33. Ibid., 126.
34. Ibid., 83–84.
35. Santayana, 'The Last Puritan', quoted in M. Tolpin, 'The Daedalus Experience: A Developmental Vicissitude of the Grandiose Fantasy', *Annual of Psychoanalysis*, 2, 1974, 216.
36. *Glimpses*, 265.
37. Rajneesh, *Books I Have Loved*, 116.
38. *Glimpses*, 88. Although Rajneesh translates *karar* as 'trust' at this particular place, he later (p.114) holds 'passionate love'—the word used here for *karar*—to be more appropriate.
39. Ibid., 111.
40. Cit. in the authorized biography by V. Joshi, *The Awakened One,* San Francisco: Harper & Row, 1982, 22–23. In Rajneesh's other accounts of the event, the grandfather is not in a coma but, with his head in the boy's lap as the bullock cart rattles along, carries out long philosophical discussions on death and attachment (cf. *Glimpses*, 79ff.). Wendy Doniger in a personal communication notes that the scene is also very much like the Upanishadic descriptionof the pranas and then the senses leaving one by one.

41. See J.B. Menes, 'Children's Reactions to the Death of a Parent: A Review of the Psychoanalytic Literature', *Journal of the American Psychoanalytic Association*, **13**, 1971, 697–719; see also, M. Wolfenstein, 'How Is Mourning Possible?', *Psychoanalytic Study of the Child*, **21**, 1966, 93–123.
42. Cited in Milne, op. cit., 96. See also the confirmatory account by Joshi, 31.
43. F. Fitzgerald, 'Rajneeshpuram-I', *The New Yorker*, 22 September 1986, 86.
44. Cited in D. Aberbach, 'Grief and Mysticism', *International Review of Psychoanalysis*, **14**, 1987, 509.
45. Ibid.
46. Joshi, op. cit., 52–53.
47. See H. Kohut, 'Forms and Transformations of Narcissism', *Journal of the American Psychoanalytic Association,* **14**, 1966, 243–72. See also Tolpin, 213–28.
48. Joshi, op. cit., 51.
49. Ibid., 61.

Seduction and the Saint: The Legend of Drukpa Kunley

1. K. Dowman and S. Paljor, *The Divine Madman: The Sublime Life and Songs of Drukpa Kunley,* Middletown, CA: The Dawn Horse Press, 1998.
2. C.G. Jung, 'Ueber den indischen Heiligen', in Zur Psychologie westlicher und oestlicher Religionen, *Gesammelte Werke*, Vol. 11, Olten: Walter-Verlag, 1976. (Translated by the author.)
3. Dowman and Paljor, op. cit., 8–9.
4. Ibid., 9.
5. Ibid., 4.
6. Ibid., 33.
7. Ibid., xxvi.
8. J. Gyatso, *Apparitions of the Self: The Secret Autobiogra-*

phies of a Tibetan Visionary, Princeton: Princeton University Press, 1998, 111.

9.   C. Trungpa, *Born in Tibet,* London: Allen and Unwin, 1985, 53.

10. E. Torres, 'A Perversion Named Desire', *International Journal of Psychoanalysis,* **72**, 1991, 83.

11. Dowman and Paljor, op. cit., 98.

12. The Thunderbolt.

13. Dowman and Paljor, op. cit., 10.

14. Ibid., 90–91.

15. Ibid., 27.

16. E.H. Erikson, *Childhood and Society,* New York: Norton, 1952.

17. A. Phillips, *On Flirtation,* Cambridge, MA: Harvard University Press, 1994, 22.

18. Dowman and Paljor, op. cit., 9.

19. S. Kakar, 'Maternal Enthrallment: Two Case Histories', in *Culture and Psyche,* Delhi: Oxford University Press, 1996, 74.

20. Swami Muktananda, *Play of Consciousness: A Spiritual Autobiography,* South Fallsburg, NY: Syda Foundation, 1994.

21. Ibid., 107.

22. Ibid., 107–08.

23. Ibid., 110–11.

24. Ibid., 116–17.

25. Ibid., 125.

26. Freud, 'A Difficulty in the Path of Psycho-analysis', *SE,* **17**, 141–42.

27. A. Vergote, *Guilt and Desire,* New Haven: Yale University Press, 1988, 174.

28. Ibid., 182.

29. H. Kramer and J. Springer, *Malleus Maleficarum,* London: Pushkin Press, 1952, 58.

30. B. Grunberger, 'The Oedipal Conflict of the Analyst', *Psychoanalytic Quarterly,* **49**, 1980, 606–30.

31. Muktananda, xiii.
32. Ibid.
33. See S. Caldwell, 'The Heart of the Secret: A Personal and Scholarly Encounter with Shakta Tantrism in Siddha Yoga', *Nova Religio*, 5(1), 2001, 9–51.
34. Freud (1915), 'A Case of Paranoia Running Counter to the Psycho-analytic Theory of the Disease', *SE*, **14**.
35. J. Laplanche, 'Seduction, Persecution, Revelation', *International Journal of Psychoanalysis*, **76**, 1995, 663–82.
36. Ibid., 659–60.
37. Ibid., 664.
38. A. Silber, 'Childhood Seduction, Parental Pathology and Hysterical Symptomatology: The Genesis of an Altered State of Consciousness',*International Journal of Psychoanalysis*, **60**, 1979, 109–16. The memories of real maternal seduction emerge reluctantly during analysis in the face of what often seems like an implacable resistance. They come up in isolated fractions, never as the coherent narrative. One of my own patients, whom I have called Pran elsewhere, has been struggling with and against the emergence of such memories over hundreds of hours and we are still uncertain on the details and extent of his seduction during adolescence. Pran exhibits a very similar pattern to that of Silber's analysand. During his sessions, dominated almost without exception by his recollections and obsessive ruminations about his mother and the afternoon naps he took with her in her bed, he too fleetingly enters an altered state of consciousness from which he emerges after several seconds feeling refreshed and invigorated. It is now apparent to both of us that one of Pran's strongest motivations to continue analysis is to experience this fugue-like state under the paternal protection of the guru-analyst and that there is an overpowering unconscious resistance working against the relinquishing of this state through remembering; see my, 'Clinical Work

and Cultural Imagination', *Psychoanalytic Quarterly,* **64**, 1995, 265–81.

39. Let me draw the reader's attention to another mother–son scene that, too, is regarded pivotal in the spiritual journey of a saint who is far away in time and space from the Hindu and Buddhist saints I have talked of so far. It is a scene where the mother and son share a mystical ecstatic experience which, though not as frankly sexual as the ones we have discussed above, will nevertheless strike a psycho-analytically sensitive reader as passionately orgiastic in its rhythm, flow and imagery. The son is St Augustine and the mother is Monica, and the scene is famous in Catholic mystical tradition as the 'Vision at Ostia' where mother and son are leaning together in a window overlooking the garden, 'discoursing together, alone, very sweetly' about eternal life. 'And when our discourse was brought to that point, that the very highest delight of the earthly senses, in the very purest material light, was, in respect of the sweet-ness of that life, not only not worthy of comparison, but not even of mention; we raising up ourselves with a more glowing affection towards the "Selfsame", did by degrees pass through all things bodily, even the very heaven whence sun and moon and stars shine upon the earth; yea, we were soaring higher yet, by inward musing, and discourse, and admiring of Thy works; and we came to our own minds, and went beyond them . . . And while we were discours-ing and panting after her, we slightly touched on her with the whole effort of our heart; and we sighed, and there we leave bound the first fruits of the Spirit; and returned to vo-cal expressions of our mouth, where the word spoken has beginning and end'; see St Augustine, *The Confessions,* R. O'Connell (ed.), Oxford: Clarendon Press, 1992, Bk. 9.10. See also, D. Capps and J. Dittes (eds), *The Hunger of the Heart: Reflections on the Confessions of Augustine,* West

Lafayette, IN: Society for the Scientific Study of Religion, Monograph Series # 8, 1990, 107–08.

Desire and the Spiritual Quest: the Legend of Drukpa Kunley (Contd)

1. Dowman and Paljor, op. cit., 10.
2. For this discussion of sexuality in Buddhism, I am indebted to Stephen Butterfield, *The Double Mirror: A Skeptical Journey into Buddhist Tantra*, Berkeley: North Atlantic Books, 1994, Ch. 9.
3. S. Kakar and J.M. Ross, *Tales of Love, Sex and Danger*, New York: Blackwell, 1986, 3.
4. St Teresa of Avila, *The Way of Perfections*, A. Peers (ed.), New York: Doubleday, 1964, 70–71.
5. Dowman and Paljor, op. cit., 123–24.
6. Kate Wheeler, 'Toward a New Spiritual Ethic', *Nexus*, March/April 1994, www.cyberpass.net/truth, 1–7.
7. Ibid., 5.
8. Butterfield, op. cit., 194.
9. Dowman and Paljor, op. cit., 67–68.
10. Phallus is a Freudian term historically related to the penis but, as a signifier, applicable to other structures of power.
11. For a discussion of the oral imagery in the Odyssey see B. Simon, 'The Hero as an Only Child: An Unconscious Fantasy Structuring Homer's Odyssey,' *International Journal of Psychoanalysis*, 55, 1974, 555–62.
12. Dowman and Paljor, op. cit., 37–38.
13. Ibid., 61.
14. Ibid., 64.
15. Ibid., 81.
16. Ibid., 104.
17. Ibid., 135.

18. Ibid., 119.
19. Ibid., 120.
20. Ibid., 122.
21. J.S. Grotstein, 'Wilfred R. Bion: The Man, the Psycho-analyst, the Mystic. A Perspective on His Life and Work', *Contemporary Psychoanalysis*, **17**, 1981, 507.
22. *Confessions*, 3.6.
23. Plato, 'Phaedrus' in J.M. Cooper (ed.), *Plato: Complete Works*, Indianapolis: Hacket, 1997, 253d.
24. J. Mascaro (ed.), *The Dhammapada*, Harmondsworth: Penguin, 1973, Verse 326.
25. Swami Vivekananda, *The Yogas and Other Works*, S. Nikhilananda (ed.), New York: Ramakrishna-Vivekananda Center, 1953, 608–09.

Gandhi and the Art of Practical Spirituality

1. M.K. Gandhi, CD of *The Collected Works of Mahatma Gandhi*, New Delhi: Government of India, Publications Division, 1999, Vol. 43, 9. (Hereafter referred to as *CWMG*.)
2. Ibid.
3. M.K. Gandhi, *An Autobiography or The Story of My Experiments with Truth*, Ahmedabad: Navajivan, 1927, xvi.
4. *CWMG*, 34, 293.
5. E.H. Erikson, *Gandhi's Truth*, New York: W.W. Norton, 1969.
6. *CWMG*, 55, 147.
7. Gandhi, *Autobiography*, 207.
8. Cited in J.A. Knight, 'The Spiritual as a Creative Force in the Person', *Journal of the American Academy of Psychoanalysis*, **15**, 1987, 365.
9. Cited in P. French, *The World Is What It Is*, London: Picador, 2008, 403.

10. Ibid., 389.
11. 'Aate hain ghaib se ye mazamiin khyal mein / Ghalib sareere-khama navaye-sarosh hai'; Personal communication from Abid Hussain, Shimla, September 2007.
12. Knight, op. cit., 368.
13. *CWMG*, 40, 14.
14. *CWMG*, 55, 147.
15. *CWMG*, 56, 286.
16. *CWMG*, 36, 5.
17. *CWMG*, 40, 1.
18. B.J. Seelig and L.S. Rosof, 'Normal and Pathological Altruism', *Journal of the American Psychoanalytic Association*, **49**, 2001, 933–59.
19. T. Singer et al., 'Empathy for Pain Involves the Affective but Not the Sensory Components of Pain', *Science*, **303**, 2004, 1157–62.
20. J. Haidt, *The Happiness Hypothesis*, New York: Basic Books, 2005, 198.
21. F. Warnecken and M. Tomasello, 'Altruistic Helping in Human Infants and Young Chimpanzees', *Science*, **311**, 2006, 1301–03.
22. *CWMG*, 19, 322.
23. *CWMG*, 43, 7.
24. D.C. Schindler, 'The Redemption of Eros: Philosophical Reflections on Benedict XVI's First Encyclical', *Communio*, **33**, 2006, 389.
25. Ibid., 390.
26. *CWMG*, 63, 348.
27. *CWMG*, 43, 8.
28. R.F. Baumeister, C. Smart and J.M. Boden, 'Relation of Threatened Egotism to Violence and Aggression: The Dark Side of High Self-esteem', *Psychological Review*, **103**, 1996, 5–33. See also R.F. Baumeister, *Evil: Inside Human Cruelty and Violence*, New York: Freeman, 1997.

29. M. Desai, *The Gita According to Gandhi*, Ahmedabad: Navajivan, 1946, 125–34.

30. Ibid., 131.

31. Ibid., 132.

32. *CWMG*, 24, 411.

33. *CWMG*, 43, 9.

34. Erikson, *Gandhi's Truth*, 412.

35. J. Jaynes, *The Origin of Consciousness in the Breakdown of the Bicameral Mind*, New York: Mariner Books, 1990, 44.

36. *CWMG*, 70, 141.

37. *CWMG*, 55, 27.

38. S. Kakar, 'Gandhi and Women', *Intimate Relations*, New Delhi: Viking, 1986, 85–128.

39. N. Bose, *My Days with Gandhi*, Kolkata: Nishana, 1953, 52.

40. *CWMG*, 94, 36.

41. *CWMG*, 94, 37.

42. For a discussion of these experiments, see also Erikson, *Gandhi's Truth*, 404–05.

43. R. Gandhi, 'Two Cheers for Tolerance', *IIC Quarterly*, Summer 2007, 146–51.

Empathy in Psychoanalysis and Spiritual Healing

1. See also, H.R. Brickman, 'The Psychoanalytic Cure and Its Discontents: A Zen Buddhist Perspective on "Common Unhappiness" and the Polarized Self', *Psychoanalysis and Contemporary Thought*, 21, 1998, 3–32.

2. Some of these are J.W. Jones, *Contemporary Psychoanalysis and Religion*, New Haven: Yale University Press, 1991; S. Kakar, *The Analyst and the Mystic*, Chicago: University of Chicago Press, 1991; W.W. Meissner, *Psychoanalysis and Religious Experience*, New Haven: Yale University Press,

1984; A.M. Rizzuto, *The Birth of the Living God*, Chicago: University of Chicago Press, 1979; A. Vergote, *Guilt and Desire*, New Haven: Yale University Press, 1988.

3. A. Newberg, et al., *Why God Won't Go Away: Brain Science and the Biology of Belief*, New York: Random House, 2001.

4. See F. Alexander, 'Buddhist Training as an Artificial Catatonia', *Psychoanalytic Review*, **18**, 1931, 129–45; S. Freud (1927), 'The Future of an Illusion' and (1930), 'Civilization and Its Discontents', *SE*, 21; H. Fingarette, 'Ego and Mythic Selflessness', *Psychoanalytic Review*, **45**, 1958, 5–40; E. Jones (1923), 'The Nature of Autosuggestion', in *Papers on Psychoanalysis*, Boston: Beacon Press, 1961, 273–93; J.M. Masson, *The Oceanic Feeling: The Origins of Religious Sentiment in Ancient India*, Dordrecht: Reidel, 1980; N. Ross, 'Affect as Cognition: With Observations on the Meaning of Mystical States', *International Review of Psycho-Analysis*, **2**, 1975, 79–93.

5. See, for instance, E. Fromm, 'Psychoanalysis and Zen Buddhism', in *Zen Buddhism and Psychoanalysis*, D.T. Suzuki, E. Fromm and R. De Martino (eds), New York: Harper, 1960, 77–141; P.C. Horton, 'The Mystical Experience: Substance of an Illusion', *Journal of the American Psychoanalytic Association*, **22**, 1974, 364–80; M. Shafii, 'Silence in Service of the Ego: Psychoanalytic Study of Meditation', *International Journal of Psychoanalysis*, **45**, 1973, 431–43; Brickman, op. cit.; Meissner, op. cit.

6. Sri Aurobindo (1911), 'Yogic Sadhan', *Sri Aurobindo Archives and Research*, **10**(1), 1986, 55–83.

7. See M. Epstein, 'Beyond the Oceanic Feeling', *International Review of Psycho-Analysis*, **17**, 1990, 159–64.

8. S. Kakar, *Shamans, Mystics and Doctors*, New York: Knopf, 1982; Kakar, *The Analyst and the Mystic*, op. cit.

9. L.L. Hallstrom, *Mother of Bliss: Anandamayi Ma,* Delhi: Oxford University Press, 1999, 10.

10. P. Jayakar, *J. Krishnamurti: A Biography,* Delhi: Penguin, 1987, 211.

11. H. Kohut, *The Analysis of the Self,* New York: International Universities Press, 1971; *The Restoration of the Self,* New York: International Universities Press, 1977; *How Analysis Cures,* Chicago: University of Chicago Press, 1984.

12. Selfobjects are those 'Others' (and their symbolic equivalents) who are deeply internalized and experienced as part of one's own self.

13. M. Kalton, 'Self transformation in the Confucian Tradition', *Psychotherapy East and West,* Seoul: Korean Academy of Psychotherapists, 1995.

14. M. Agarwal, *Sai Ek, Roop Anek* ('Sai is one but forms are many'), Kolkata: Sri Satya Sai Book and Publications Trust, 2000, 54.

15. Ibid., 116.

16. Kakar, *The Analyst and the Mystic,* Ch. 3.

17. Swami Muktananda, *The Perfect Relationship,* Ganeshpuri: Gurudev Siddha Vidyapeeth, 1983, 3.

18. Kakar, *The Analyst and the Mystic,* 52.

19. Agarwal, 72.

20. W. James, *The Varieties of Religious Experience,* op. cit., 102.

21. Ibid., 176.

22. D. Nurbakhsh, 'Sufism and Psychoanalysis', *International Journal of the Society of Psychiatrists,* **24**, 1978, 208.

23. Agarwal, op. cit., 7.

24. Ibid., 28.

25. Ibid., 29–30.

26. I. Grubrich-Simitis, 'Six Letters of Sigmund Freud and Sándor Ferenczi on the Interrelationship of Psycho-analytic

Theory and Technique', *International Review of Psycho-Analysis*, **13**, 1986, 271.

27. G. Satran, 'Some Limits and Hazards of Empathy', *Contemporary Psychoanalysis*, **27**, 1991, 739.

28. Freud (1923), 'Two Encyclopaedia Articles', *SE*, **18**, 239.

29. A. Ehrenzweig, 'The Undifferentiated Matrix of Artistic Identification', in *The Psychoanalytic Study of Society*, Vol. 3, W. Muensterberger and S. Axelrad (eds), New York: International Universities Press, 1964.

30. T. Ogden, 'Reverie and Metaphor', *International Journal of Psychoanalysis*, **78**, 1997, 719–32.

31. Ibid., 719.

32. Roazen in H. Deutsch, 'On Satisfaction, Happiness and Ecstasy', *International Journal of Psychoanalysis*, **70**, 1989, 715.

33. Freud (1927), 'The Future of an Illusion', *SE*, **21**, 31–32.

34. H. Deutsch, 'Okkulte Vorgaenge waehrend der Psychoanalyse', *Imago*, **12**, 1926, 418–33.

35. C. Rycroft, 'Review of G. Devereux (ed) "Psychoanalysis and the Occult"', *International Journal of Psychoanalysis*, **35**, 1954, 70–71.

36. S. Levy, 'Empathy and Psychoanalytic Technique', *Journal of the American Psychoanalytic Association*, **33**, 1985, 353–78.

37. Grubrich-Simitis, op. cit., 272.

38. G. Pigman, 'Freud and the History of Empathy', *International Journal of Psychoanalysis*, **76**, 1995, 237–56.

39. Levy, op. cit., 356.

40. A. Reich, 'Empathy and Countertransference', in *Psychoanalytic Contributions*, New York: International Universities Press, 1973, 344–60.

41. R. Schaefer, 'Generative Empathy in the Treatment Situation', *Psychoanalytic Quarterly*, **28**, 1959, 342.

42. H. Kohut, 'Introspection, Empathy and Psychoanalysis',

Journal of the American Psychoanalytic Association, 7, 1959, 459.

43. R. Greenson, 'Empathy and Its Vicissitudes', *International Journal of Psychoanalysis*, **41**, 1960, 418.

44. Freud (1912–13), 'Totem and Taboo', *SE*, **13**, 103.

45. See D. Buie, 'Empathy: Its Nature and Limitations', *Journal of the American Psychoanalytic Association*, **30**, 1981, 959–78; I. Moses, 'The Misuse of Empathy in Psychoanalysis', *Contemporary Psychoanalysis*, **24**, 1988, 577–94; T. Shapiro, 'The Development and Distortions of Empathy', *Psychoanalytic Quarterly*, **43**, 1974, 4–25; D. Spence, 'Discussion of I. Moses: The Misuse of Empathy in Psychoanalysis', *Contemporary Psychoanalysis*, **24**, 1988, 594–98; R. Tuch, 'Beyond Empathy: Concerning Certain Complexities in the Self Psychology Theory', *Psychoanalytic Quarterly*, **66**, 1997, 259–82.

46. Satran, op. cit., 739.

47. Spence, op. cit., 596.

48. Satran, op. cit., 739.

49. Greenson, op. cit., 420.

50. But see T.J. Jacobs, 'Posture, Gesture and Movement in the Analyst: Cues to Interpretation and Countertransference', *Journal of the American Psychoanalytic Association*, **21**, 1973, 72–92; 'Non-verbal Communications: Some Reflections on their Role in the Psychoanalytic Process and Psychoanalytic Education', *Journal of the American Psychoanalytic Association*, **42**, 1994, 741–62; 'When the Body Speaks: Psychoanalytic Meaning in Kinetic Clues', *Psychoanalytic Quarterly*, **64**, 1995, 784–88.

51. R. Spitz, *No and Yes*, New York: International Universities Press, 1957.

52. J.M. Ross, 'The Fate of Relatives and Colleagues in the Aftermath of Boundary Violations', *Journal of the American Psychoanalytic Association*, **43**, 1995, 959–61.

53. Jayakar, op. cit., 8.
54. Muktananda, op. cit., 37.
55. Brickman, op. cit.
56. J. Keats, *Letters of John Keats*, H.E. Rollins (ed.), Cambridge, MA: Harvard University Press, 1958, 193.
57. S. Leavy, 'John Keats' Psychology of Creative Imagination', *Psychoanalytic Quarterly*, **39**, 1970, 173–97.
58. Hallstrom, op. cit., 98.
59. Ibid., 26.
60. W.C. Chittick, *The Sufi Path of Love: The Spiritual Teachings of Rumi*, Albany: SUNY Press, 1983, 145.
61. Keats, op. cit., 386–87.
62. W.R. Bion, 'Notes on Memory and Desire', *Psychoanalytic Forum*, **2**, 1967, 271–80.
63. Aurobindo, op. cit.
64. J.S. Grotstein, 'Wilfred R. Bion: The Man, the Psychoanalyst, the Mystic. A Perspective on His Life and Work', *Contemporary Psychoanalysis*, **17**, 1981, 501–36.
65. S. Bolognini, 'Empathy and the Unconscious', *Psychoanalytic Quarterly*, **70**, 2001, 447–71.
66. Dalai Lama in 'Workshop on Buddhism', op. cit.

The Uses of Ritual

1. P. Ricouer, *Freud and Philosophy: An Essay in Interpretation*, New Haven: Yale University Press, 1970, 33.
2. M. Douglas, *Purity and Danger*, London: Routledge and Kegan Paul, 1966; R.A. Rapaport, 'The Obvious Aspects of Ritual', in *Ecology, Meaning and Religion*, Berkeley, CA: North Atlantic Books, 1979, 175–221.
3. S. Kakar, *Shamans, Mystics and Doctors*, New York: Knopf, 1982, Chs 3 and 4.
4. S. Caldwell, *Oh Terrifying Mother: Sexuality, Violence and*

Worship of the Goddess Kali, New York: Oxford University Press, 2001.

5.   W.B. Yeats, *The Collected Poems of W.B. Yeats*, New York: Macmillan, 1956, 287.

6.   P. Ricouer, *The Symbol of Evil*, E. Buchanan (tr.), New York: Harper & Row, 1969, 349.

Religion and Psyche: Reading Freud's 'The Future of an Illusion' in Goa

1.   S. Freud (1927), 'The Future of an Illusion', *SE*, **21**, 7.

2.   F. Nietzsche, *The Use and Abuse of History*, Indianapolis: Bobbs Merrill, 1949.

3.   C. Taylor, *Philosophical Arguments*, Cambridge, MA: Harvard University Press, 1995, 70.

4.   For some exceptions see E.H. Erikson, 'On the Nature of Psycho-historical Evidence', in Erikson (ed.), *Life History and the Historical Moment*, New York: Norton, 1975; R. Stolorow and G. Atwood, *Contexts of Being*, Hillsdale, NJ: Analytic Press, 1992; R. Stolorow, D. Orange and G. Atwood, 'World Horizons: A Post-Cartesian Alternative to the Freudian Unconscious', *Contemporary Psychoanalysis*, **37**, 2001, 43–61.

5.   M. Heidegger, *Being and Time,* New York: Harper & Row, 1927; H.G. Gadamer, *Truth and Method*, New York: Crossword, 1975; W. Dilthey, 'The Types of World View and Their Development in Metaphysical Systems', in Dilthey, *Selected Writings*, H.P. Rickman (ed.), Cambridge: Cambridge University Press, 1976.

6.   See T.J. Zeddies, 'Behind, Beneath, Above, and Beyond', *Journal of the American Academy of Psychoanalysis*, **30**, 2002, 211–29.

7.   'The Future of an Illusion', 7–8.

8. H. Loewald, 'Review of the Freud/Jung Letters', *Psychoanalytic Quarterly*, **46**, 1977, 514–27.

9. C.E. Schorske, *Fin-de-siècle Vienna: Politics and Culture*, New York: Knopf, 1979; W.J. McGrath, *Freud's Discovery of Psychoanalysis*, Ithaca: Cornell University Press, 1986; P. Gay, *Freud: A Life for Our Time*, New York: Norton, 1988.

10. O. Pfister, 'The Illusion of a Future: A Friendly Disagreement with Prof. Sigmund Freud', *International Journal of Psychoanalysis*, **74**, 1993, 557–58.

11. A. Rizzuto, *Why Did Freud Reject God? A Psychodynamic Interpretation*, New Haven, CT: Yale University Press, 1998. See also M. Ostow, 'A Godless Jew', *International Review of Psychoanalysis*, **16**, 1998, 119–21.

12. S. Freud, 'Letter from Sigmund Freud to Sándor Ferenczi, October 23, 1927', in *The Correspondence of Sigmund Freud and Sándor Ferenczi*, Vol. 3, 1920–33, 75.

13. S. Freud (1930), 'Civilization and Its Discontents', *SE*, **21**, 74.

14. Ibid., 74.

15. G. Flood, *An Introduction to Hinduism*, Cambridge: Cambridge University Press, 1998, 199.

16. A. Michaels, *Hinduismus*, Munich: C.H. Beck, 1998, 17–18.

17. 'The Future of an Illusion', 17.

18. S. Radhakrishnan, *The Principal Upanishads*, New Delhi: HarperCollins, 1994, 235.

19. S. Kakar, *The Inner World: A Psychoanalytic Study of Childhood and Society in India*, Delhi and New York: Oxford University Press, 1982, 200–04.

20. Ibid., 110

21. Cited in W. [Doniger] O'Flaherty, *Women, Androgynes and Other Mythical Beasts*, Chicago: University of Chicago Press, 1980, 91.

22. S. Kakar, *The Analyst and the Mystic* (Chicago: University of Chicago Press, 1992), 17–18.

23. M. Foucault, *The Archaeology of Knowledge*, A. Sheridan Smith (tr.), London: Tavistock Publications, 1972.

24. 'The Future of an Illusion', 43.

25. K. Subramaniam, *Srimad Bhagavatam*, Mumbai: Bharatiya Vidya Bhavan, 1988, 330–31.

26. W. [Doniger] O'Flaherty, *Dreams, Illusions and Other Realities*, Chicago: University of Chicago Press, 1984, 118.

27. See D. W. Winnicott, 'Transitional Objects and Transitional Phenomena', in *Through Paediatrics to Psycho-Analysis*, New York: Basic Books, 1975, 229–42; and Winnicott, 'Living Creatively', in *Home Is Where We Start From*, Harmondsworth: Pelican Books, 1986.

28. W.W. Meissner, 'Religious Thinking as Transitional Conceptualization', *Psychoanalhytical Review*, 79, 1992, 175–96; P. Pruyser, *The Play of the Imagination: Toward a Psychoanalysis of Culture*, New York: International Universities Press, 1983; A. Rizzuto, *The Birth of the Living God: A Psychoanalytic Study*, Chicago: University of Chicago Press, 1979.

29. 'The Future of an Illusion', 29.

30. W. [Doniger] O'Flaherty, *Dreams, Illusions and Other Realities*, 118.

31. For a summary of these ideas see, M. Arden, 'Psychoanalysis and Survival', *International Journal of Psychoanalysis*, 66, 1985, 471–80.

32. W. Shakespeare, *The Tempest*, IV:i:156–57.

33. W. [Doniger] O'Flaherty, *Dreams, Illusions and Other Realities*, 119.

34. Ibid., 126.

35. K. Popper, *Objective Knowledge: An Evolutionary Approach*, Oxford: Oxford University Press, 1979, 37.

36. *Future of an Illusion*, 53.

37. P. Mahony, *Freud as a Writer*, New York: International Universities Press, 1982, 11–12.
38. G. Papini (1969), 'A Visit to Freud'. *Review of Existential Psychology and Psychiatry*, 9, 130–34, cited in E. Gomez, 'Some Psychoanalytical Thoughts about King Lear, Dante and Don Quixote', *Journal of the American Academy of Psychoanalysis*, 14, 1986, 545.

Afterword: Spirit and Psyche

1. A. Calaprice (ed.), *The Expanded Quotable Einstein*, Princeton: Princeton University Press, 2000, 10.
2. G. Rose, *Necessary Illusion: Art as Witness*, Madison, CT: International Universities Press, 1996, 58.
3. Cited in S.A. Leavy, 'John Keats's Psychology of Creative Imagination', *Psychoanalytic Quarterly*, 39, 1970, 176.
4. Ibid., 174.
5. Ibid., 178
6. G. Flaubert cit. in A. Marguiles, 'The Empathic Imagination', *Journal of the American Academy of Psychoanalysis*, 21, 1993, 516.

ACKNOWLEDGEMENTS

$\mathcal{M}$y greatest debt of gratitude is to my wife, Katharina Kakar, who was not only a source of support and encouragement but who discussed and actively contributed to refining some of the ideas presented in this book. I also thank my old friend Wendy Doniger, for taking out time to read and comment on the manuscript. Some of these essays, extensively revised for this book, were presented as talks and later published in different places.

'Empathy in Psychoanalysis and Spiritual Healing' was first delivered as 'The Freud Lecture' of the Sigmund Freud Foundation in Frankfurt, Germany, on 1 November 2001. A revised version was delivered as the 'Ninth Kardiner Award Lecture' of the Psychoanalytic Training and Research Institute of Columbia University on 2 April 2002 and was published in the *Journal of Analytical Psychology*, 48, 2003.

'Seduction and the Saint' appeared in the *Annual for Psychoanalysis*, 31, 2003.

'Gandhi and the Art of Practical Spirituality' was first given as the inaugural lecture of the series 'Masters of Indian Spirituality' organized by the Udo Keller Foundation Forum Humanum at Neversdorf, Germany, on 19 June 2007.

'The Uses of Ritual' was the inaugural lecture at the 'International Conference on Ritual', New Delhi, 11–14 October 2006 and will be published in C. Brosius and U. Huesken (eds), *Ritual Matters* by Routledge South Asia.

'Reading Freud's "The Future of an Illusion in Goa"' was prepared for the International Psychoanalytic Association's monograph series, 'Contemporary Freud: Turning Points and Critical Issues', and will be published in S. Akhtar (ed.), *On Freud's 'The Future of an Illusion'*, New Haven: Yale University Press.